menagerie
rare theatre well done

Menagerie Theatre presents

CW00433902

Frobisher's Gold

or *Elizabeth the First Had Black Teeth*
by Fraser Grace

A heart of ice, a glimmer of gold, love, betrayal...
and the perils of bad teeth!

First performed at The Junction, Cambridge on Thursday 19 October 2006

Frobisher's Gold

by Fraser Grace

Elizabeth Janet Suzman
Martin Frobisher Darren Strange
William Crowe Patrick Morris
Walsingham Terry Molloy
Robert Devereux / Mr Walker Jamie Belman
Bo'sun / Dr Burcot Denis Quilligan
Ship's Boy Caroline Rippin

Director Paul Bourne
Associate Director Rachel Aspinwall
Set Design Richard Matthews
Video Design Chris Rogers
Original Music & Sound Design Scott Myers
Lighting Design Sherry Coenen
Costume Design Alexandra Kharibian
General Manager Alex Drury

Biographies

Writer

Fraser Grace

Before becoming a playwright Fraser worked as an actor and performance poet.

His first play *Perpetua* – about the US 'abortion wars' – was joint winner of the Verity Bargate Award in 1996, produced at Birmingham REP in 1999, and revived in 2004 at the Latchmere Theatre, Battersea. More recent productions include *Gifts of War* for Menagerie Theatre, and *Bubble*, a collaborative project with the poet Andrea Porter, broadcast by BBC Radio 4 in October 2004.

Who Killed Mr Drum?, based on the memoir by Sylvester Stein and co-written with the author, ran for eight weeks at the Riverside Studios in 2005 in a production by Treatment Theatre. *Breakfast with Mugabe* was produced at the Swan Theatre, Stratford by the Royal Shakespeare Company and directed by Sir Antony Sher in October 2005. The production transferred to Soho Theatre in April 2006, and opened at the Duchess Theatre, West End in May 2006. The production was also broadcast on BBC Radio 3. The play was recently named joint winner of the 2006 John Whiting Award.

Fraser is currently writing an opera with the composer Andrew Lovett, and is also under commission at the National Theatre. He is an Associate Writer for Menagerie Theatre Company, who commissioned *Frobisher's Gold* in December 2003.

Cast

Elizabeth **Janet Suzman**

After graduating from The University of the Witwatersrand, Janet came to the UK to train at LAMDA, and shortly after leaving joined the Royal Shakespeare Company for their quatercentenary season, *The Wars of the Roses*, going on to play many of the major roles, culminating in a 'thrilling account' by Trevor Nunn in 1973 of *Antony and Cleopatra*. In 1980 she returned to the RSC for Clytemnaestra and Helen of Troy in John Barton's all-day decathlon *The Greeks*. Janet has twice won the Evening Standard Best Actress Award, for *Three Sisters* and Fugard's *Hello and Goodbye*.

Janet retains close links with her native country and in 1976 opened The Market Theatre with *The Death of Bessie Smith*, directed by the late Barney Simon, with John Kani and Winston Ntshona. She directed Kani in *Othello* in 1987 and filmed it for Channel 4 TV. A decade later she returned to direct her version of Brecht's *Good Person of Setzuan*, written in collaboration with Gcina Mhlophe, re-titled *The Good Woman of Sharkville*. In 1997 her version of *The Cherry Orchard* aka *The Free State* played at Birmingham and won the Barclays TMA Best Director Award.

Films include: *Nicholas and Alexandra* (Academy Award and Golden Globe Best Actress Nominations), *A Day in the Death of Joe Egg* with the late Alan Bates, Peter Greenaway's *The Draughtsman's Contract*, *The Priest of Love* (with Ian McKellen and the late Ava Gardner), *A Dry White Season* with Donald Sutherland, Fellini's *And The Boat Sails On*, and a handful of comedies. TV includes: Arnold Bennet's Clayhanger trilogy, *Mountbatten – Last*

Viceroy of India and Dennis Potter's *The Singing Detective*.

Following *Frobisher's Gold*, Janet will appear in the RSC's *Coriolanus*, the last play of the Complete Works Festival. Her production of *Hamlet* from SA was the first, so you may say she book-ends the Festival.

Martin Frobisher
Darren Strange

A regular performer in *The Armando Iannucci Shows*, other television & film credits include: *One Free Hand, Noah's Ark, London Bridge, London's Burning, Innocents, Human Remains, Let's Be Clear About This, One Free Hand, 2004 The Stupid Version, Casualty, Judge John Deed.* Theatre includes: *Talk Of The City, The Tempest, Two Gentlemen Of Verona* (RSC). *The Old Curiosity Shop* (Southwark Playhouse). *A Box Of Bananas* (Gate Theatre). UK tours of *Cat On A Hot Tin Roof, The Misanthrope, The Wedding, Romeo & Juliet. Don Quixote* (Merlin Theatre, Hungary).

Darren has also written television sketches and additional material for *The Armstrong & Miller Show* and *Bruiser*, a radio comedy *None Shall Pass* and his own plays *The Year Of The Bag, The Man Who Wanted To Become, Lookalike.*

William Crowe   Patrick Morris

Patrick was most recently seen in *Clare's Walk*, a one-man show by Steve Waters inspired by the poet John Clare's legendary journey from Epping Forest to his home village near Peterborough. Work for Menagerie includes *06/07/05* and *The Cull* by Steve Waters and *Hard Sell* by Craig Baxter. He has toured nationally with Foursight Theatre in *Medea* and *Pushing Daisies* and off-Broadway shows in the USA include *Henry VI* at the Joseph Papp Public Theatre, *Counting The Ways* directed by

Joseph Chaikin, *Springtime* and *Oscar and Bertha* directed by Maria Irene Fornes and a revival of *On The Razzle* working with Tom Stoppard.

Directing credits for Menagerie include *The Retreating World* and *Between This Breath and You* by Naomi Wallace and *Correspondence* by Claire Macdonald along with new plays by Polly Wiseman, Mark Norfolk, Amanda Whittington and Craig Baxter. In 2005, he directed the premiere of Andrew Lovett's opera, *Abraham*, at The Junction in Cambridge, which will eventually tour nationally and internationally. Patrick is Associate Artistic Director of Menagerie.

Walsingham   Terry Molloy

Perhaps best known for his work on Radio, Terry won the Pye (now known as the Sony) Radio Award as Best Actor in 1981 for his portrayal of Boko in Ron Hutchinson's play *Risky City*, and in 1992 his performance as Pablo Picasso helped Radio 4 scoop the coveted Gold Medal in the New York Radio Festival for *Guernica*. In 1973 he joined the cast of *The Archers* as Mike Tucker and has played the part ever since.

Terry has appeared in many Repertory and Touring Theatre productions with parts ranging from Mr Toad in *Toad of Toad Hall* to Arturo Ui in Brecht's *The Resistible Rise of Arturo Ui*. On Television Terry is also well known to *Doctor Who* fans as Davros, creator of the Daleks, playing the Doctor's nemesis since 1983 and recently starring in a 4-part audio mini-series *I, Davros.*

Terry lives in Norfolk where he enjoys helping his wife Victoria in the garden, and tinkering with his website www.terrymolloy.co.uk

Robert Devereux / Mr Walker
Jamie Belman

Jamie graduated from The Webber Douglas Academy of Dramatic Art in July this year. He has just finished filming a new BBC 1 Drama *The Innocence*. This is Jamie's professional stage debut.

Bo'sun / Dr Burcot
Denis Quilligan

Denis's most recent roles include HH Asquith PM in RTE's *The Man who Lost Ireland* and Uncle Quagmire and Melanie Mouse for Theatre 503's *Yorgjin Oxo – The Man*. Other theatre work includes roles at Manchester Royal Exchange and Library, Glasgow Citz, Kings Head and West End, The Bush, Liverpool Playhouse, Edinburgh Lyceum, Leicester Haymarket and The Public in New York. On TV: *The Baby War, Father Ted, The Bill, Fair City, The Key* and *Minder*. On radio: *The Wexford Trilogy* and *Dubliners* by James Joyce

Ship's Boy **Caroline Rippin**

Caroline trained at Bretton Hall. Theatre credits include *Stormin' Jack Norman* (Theatre 503), *Michelle and the Landlady* (Pleasance), *Motherf**ker Island, In the White Highlands* (Drama Centre), *Peer Gynt* (Wakefield Opera House), *White Nights* (The Spot, Covent Garden). She has also toured with Classworks, Empty Hat and Open Hand. This summer Caroline made her directorial debut at The Junction with *Black Light* by Nick Harrop and *Doghead Boy and Sharkmouth go to Ikea* by Dawn King.

Production Team

Director **Paul Bourne**

Paul is Artistic Director of Menagerie Theatre Company, Cambridge, the East of England's leading independent new writing theatre company. He spent two years as the Artistic Director at Center Stage, New York, and six years as a freelance director in Germany. Credits include the European premiere of David Mamet's *Oleanna* and the world premiere of Tennessee Williams' last short play *Williams' Guignol*. For Menagerie he commissions The Hotbed new writing festival and has directed many of the company's regional and national touring productions including Pam Gien's *The Syringa Tree*, Steve Waters' *The Cull, The Gifts of War* by Fraser Grace, *Seeds* by Diane Samuels, *Sweetie Pie* by Anna Reynolds, *The Yellow Boat* by David Saar and *Hard Sell* by Craig Baxter.

Associate Director
Rachel Aspinwall

Rachel Aspinwall trained in Paris at Ecole Jacques LeCoq. She is a co-founder of Menagerie and now works with the company as actress and director. She was the dramaturg on *Frobisher's Gold* directing its first two staged readings. Directing credits include *Motherf***er Island* by Tim Etchells (Forced Entertainment), *Michelle and the Landlady* by Caroline Forbes and *Intake/Outake* for Tiebreak Theatre. Acting credits include: *Two Into War* (Peter Brook Empty Space award-winning Theatre 503), Rhiannon in *The Cull* by Steve Waters and Jessie in *'Night Mother* by Marsha Norman. She is also the director of Part Exchange, a collective of artists from different disciplines who produce cross-art form, site specific theatre with new writing at its core.

Menagerie

Menagerie is a leading independent producer of new writing for the stage. In addition to high quality commissioning and touring the company also promotes a wide range of theatre projects including the Hotbed festival.

www.menagerie.uk.com

Thanks

Thanks are due to everyone who has worked on Frobisher's Gold through development and into production. In particular, we would like to thank Korinna Röding, Alison Mitchell (RSC), Helen Gould, Lucia Hogg, Cat Moore and all at the Shaw Theatre.

Produced in association with The Junction and Shaw Theatre.

FROBISHER'S GOLD

First published in 2006 by Oberon Books Ltd
521 Caledonian Road, London N7 9RH
Tel: 020 7607 3637 / Fax: 020 7607 3629
e-mail: info@oberonbooks.com
www.oberonbooks.com

Frobisher's Gold © Fraser Grace 2006

Fraser Grace is hereby identified as author of this play in accordance with section 77 of the Copyright, Designs and Patents Act 1988. The author has asserted his moral rights.

A catalogue record for this book is available from the British Library.

ISBN: 1 84002 709 6 / 978-1-84002-709-9

Cover image: The District (www.thedistrict.co.uk)

Printed in Great Britain by Antony Rowe Ltd, Chippenham.

Characters

ELIZABETH
Queen of England, not yet a legend

ROBERT DEVEREUX
Earl of Essex, a courtier

WALSINGHAM
Elizabeth's confidant and spymaster

MARTIN FROBISHER
a pirate and explorer

WILLIAM CROWE
a surgeon and idealist

BO'SUN, SHIP'S BOY, MR WALKER
Frobisher's crew

DR BURCOT
an ancient

Where possible, SHIP'S BOY *should be played by a female actor.*

Suggested doubling:
ROBERT DEVEREUX / MR WALKER
and
BO'SUN / DR BURCOT

*The action takes place in 1577, at the Queen's palace at Windsor,
and in Friesland, in the Arctic circle.*

Ask of me, and I shall give you the heathen for thine inheritance,
and the uttermost parts of the earth for thy possession.

Psalms, II: 8

Let me have a surgeon: I am cut to the brains.

King Lear, IV: 6

Part One

1
A STRANGE COMMISSION

The Royal Palace at Windsor. A chamber. A window. Distant singing of madrigals. ELIZABETH and her much younger courtier, DEVEREUX, have been playing chess. She (inevitably) has won, but DEVEREUX is gallant in defeat.

DEVEREUX: Aaagh – you win again!

She glares at him, speaking levelly.

ELIZABETH: Do you know what bugs me, Devereux?

Beat. He sits up, leaning on one arm, complacently.

DEVEREUX: I have no idea.

(*Pulling the sweet box towards him, evading.*) Did we run out of sweets?

ELIZABETH: I am awaiting a reply, Master Devereux.

Surely you are finally sensitive to my likes and dislikes – outside the bedroom. What can Elizabeth Tudor really not abide?

He thinks.

DEVEREUX: The non-payment of taxes.

ELIZABETH: And?

DEVEREUX: I cannot tell, Your Majesty is always so sweet tempered.

ELIZABETH: Underachievement. I rule a nation of underachievers. What's worse, you take pleasure in it. You, Devereux.

DEVEREUX: Me?!! When did I disappoint my Lady? Tell me when, and how…

ELIZABETH: Oh my Lord, they are so many ways.

I did say, outside the bedroom.

You consider a failure to master a simple game of chess makes you noble. Endearing. It doesn't.

DEVEREUX: I did try. I always try, Lizzy.

ELIZABETH: Try, and fail. Underachievement.

My cousin inherits a land of olive trees and sangria. Spain is a country with only two coasts yet his ships, Philip's galleons, storm home half-sunk with gold. Stinking with it. What do I get? England. Coast is virtually all England is, yet my sailors, my brave 'seafarers', skulk around Devon smuggling brandy.

DEVEREUX: To avoid the payment of taxes, my Lady.

ELIZABETH: It won't do.

What else?

DEVEREUX: Ma'am?

ELIZABETH: What else infuriates me? It's a warm day, you've done your duty, I am dressed, the day's business yawns before us – what else drives me to distraction.

DEVEREUX: Your scalp Ma'am.

ELIZABETH: Thank you. My scalp is driving me fucking mad.

DEVEREUX: And it's not just a duty Ma'am.

ELIZABETH: Flatterer. And a good one; here – there's a sovereign for your wardrobe.

DEVEREUX: You are too generous, my Lady. Though I'd rather have a sovereign for my bed…

ELIZABETH: You'd better leave us, I've work to do.

DEVEREUX: Work, Majesty? For the Queen of England?

ELIZABETH: Ruling, Devereux. I have people to see, places to conquer, teeth to display to an island's advantage…

She flashes her smile.

DEVEREUX: Your teeth do look wonderful, Your Majesty.

ELIZABETH: Thank you, Devereux. *Aqua fortis* – nitric acid to you – hurts like hell and costs a fortune but worth it, don't you think?

DEVEREUX: So sweet a smile hath no price.

He picks up his cloak with a flourish.

Will I visit you tonight, Your Majesty?

ELIZABETH: How will I know, am I a mystic?

Same time, same bedchamber. Why not.

DEVEREUX kisses the QUEEN's hand.

DEVEREUX: 'Why not'. A perfect maxim for life.

She smiles indulgently. He makes to exit.

ELIZABETH: You'd better not leave through that door, my Lord. Walsingham has ears. Go through my bedchamber. And mind you keep mum.

DEVEREUX: Till tonight, Majesty.

He exits, just as WALSINGHAM enters through the main door, carrying a ledger. WALSINGHAM is distracted, trying to identify the man leaving. ELIZABETH employs some distraction of her own.

ELIZABETH: My dear Wally. How is your East Anglia?

WALSINGHAM: Oh. It's passable, Ma'am.

ELIZABETH: Yes, I heard that. Are those sweets you're carrying?

WALSINGHAM: They are indeed, Majesty.

ELIZABETH: The Duke of Anjou continues to pursue me then.

She takes the new box of sweets.

WALSINGHAM: Happily he does, Ma'am, though these are in fact a gift from the explorer, Captain Frobisher – he they call 'Fearless Frobisher'.

ELIZABETH: Ha! 'Feckless Frobisher' is a pirate. Still, 'twould be a crime to refuse his bounty…

WALSINGHAM: He claims to have discovered a new land, Your Majesty. Somewhere in the arctic, I believe.

ELIZABETH: Yes, I heard that too.

She recoils from the smell.

Ugggh!

She takes out a 'chocolate' and examines it.

WALSINGHAM: Seal blubber, perhaps…?

ELIZABETH's face shows her repulsion. She puts the piece back in the box.

Shall I read the list now, Ma'am?

ELIZABETH: I think you should. Before Frobisher's wanderlust infects us all.

WALSINGHAM: In addition to the Duke of Anjou – who waits, if I may say, most elegantly – their Graces the Dukes of Argyle and Rothesay petition the Queen to support them against the Pope's paythings; Sir William Cordell, your Master of the Rolls, requests your judgement concerning certain patents currently owned by the Crown; Lord Cranfield of Monmouth…

ELIZABETH: Stop. On reflection Sir Francis, another breakfast with our Master of the Rolls and we shall grow more stale than the seal blubber.

WALSINGHAM: Perhaps then it is the perfect moment for you to meet the Duke d'Anjou, who, as I say, is really quite…

ELIZABETH: No. I shall have the Frenchman wait a while longer.

WALSINGHAM: (*With patience.*) Whatever you think best, Ma'am.

ELIZABETH: I shall see the pirate.

WALSINGHAM: (*Protesting.*) But Your Majesty…

ELIZABETH: He is still here, I take it?

WALSINGHAM: Yes, Majesty, but…

ELIZABETH: Good. I shall start with him. The Age of Underachievement draws to a close, Wally. Besides, I have an account to settle with Captain Frobisher.

WALSINGHAM: At once, Ma'am.

WALSINGHAM bows and exits. ELIZABETH walks to the globe. She spins it round. While it is spinning, enter FROBISHER. Bowing deeply, with a certain swagger, though style is not his natural game. He is accompanied by CROWE, *who also bows deeply. He is very plainly dressed, in black.*

FROBISHER: At your service, Your Majesty.

Beat. ELIZABETH *looks from* FROBISHER *to* CROWE *and back again.*

ELIZABETH: (*To* WALSINGHAM.) The high seas have grown more dangerous than we thought Sir Francis: even our pirates go round in pairs.

FROBISHER: I beg Your Majesty, call us not pirates. Call us – explorers.

ELIZABETH: Ha! It is true, then. Our pirate hath relaunched himself. Who's this?

FROBISHER: Master William Crowe, Your Majesty, the physician. My partner in the present enterprise.

ELIZABETH: A physician. A scholar is always welcome here, Master Crowe. As the Captain knows, I prize the intellect above all a man's qualities. Barring honesty.

They exchange a bow.

CROWE: I do thank Your Majesty.

FROBISHER: Master Crowe and I are recently come from the Arctic, Your Majesty.

ELIZABETH: So we gather. We thank you for the seal blubber. It smells execrable.

FROBISHER: It does Majesty. And yet what is sour outside, can so oft bring forth sweetness.

ELIZABETH: I trust you are not referring to your Queen?

CROWE clears his throat.

CROWE: The Captain refers I am sure to the seal blubber, Majesty. Her Majesty being to sourness, what sunshine is to night.

ELIZABETH: (*To FROBISHER.*) So finally the pirate gets himself poetry. I hear you have found a new land too. Show me, on my globe.

FROBISHER: There, Your Majesty.

ELIZABETH examines it, standing very close, to compensate for her short-sightedness.

ELIZABETH: And you swear you thought of your queen every day of your voyage?

FROBISHER: We did, Majesty.

ELIZABETH: Yet you didn't think to call this new land 'Bethland'. 'Tudorea'. Something of that kind?

FROBISHER: Friesland seemed…appropriate.

ELIZABETH: Are you saying our name would not be appropriate?

FROBISHER: The island is called Friesland, Majesty, for the land there is extremely…freezing.

ELIZABETH: Don't humour me, Frobisher. A thing cannot be extremely freezing. It either is freezing or it is not. Is that not so, Wally?

WALSINGHAM: I think it is, Ma'am.

CROWE: And yet, the Captain does stumble on a germ of truth, Your Majesty. The name derives from the Dutch, meaning…freezing.

FROBISHER: The name can be changed, with ease. Just as soon as we secure a patron for the new voyage.

ELIZABETH: Ah, now we have it. And what makes you think Elizabeth would be your patron?

FROBISHER: We have found gold there, Majesty.

Beat. CROWE steps forward and opens the wooden box.

CROWE: Your Majesty.

ELIZABETH: What's this?

FROBISHER: Black Earth. The gold is within.

CROWE: Kept safe, Majesty, like the oyster's pearl.

ELIZABETH: It is you who found the rock?

CROWE: No, Your Majesty. That was Captain Frobisher's fortune. My own quest is an altogether less tangible treasure.

ELIZABETH: Is Master Crowe a priest?

FROBISHER: A physician, and as you say, a scholar.

CROWE: My study is humanity. I am a student of humankind.

FROBISHER: Master Crowe opened up the first Esquimaux, as I opened up the new land. From whence this Black Earth was raised.

ELIZABETH: You opened up an Esquimaux? How, 'opened up'?

CROWE: A post mortem, tracing the cause of our Esquimaux's untimely death. When Captain Frobisher landed him, in Harwich.

Beat. She picks up the rock, then asks permission.

ELIZABETH: I can handle this rock can I?

FROBISHER: Yes Majesty. Though as you see, it is heavy with its ore.

ELIZABETH: I don't *see* anything of the kind. If this is invisible gold, I shall be disappointed.

FROBISHER: The gold is real as the Spaniard's Majesty, once the dross is bled off. The assayers predict a rock this size will yield more than a pound of gold. For the sharp investor, that's good profit.

ELIZABETH: Ha!

ELIZABETH tosses the rock to FROBISHER, who works to catch it.

I do have some science. A rock cannot yield more than its own weight however precious the metal. Or did you also discover new laws of science on your travels?

FROBISHER: A pound is the upper estimate, Majesty.

ELIZABETH: Your rock is well named. I don't like black. It reminds us of decay. Gloriana, does not do decay.

She flashes her smile. CROWE is first to understand, and to react.

CROWE: We pray the rock will bring as much glitter to England, as her Majesty's smile brings to the world, Your Majesty.

Beat. ELIZABETH is suitably pacified by the thought of gold, if not the flattery.

ELIZABETH: What do you seek for this new expedition. How much?

FROBISHER: If it were possible, Your Majesty might also consider supplying a ship, or two ships…

ELIZABETH: I have supplied ships to you before, Captain. As I recall, you lost them.

FROBISHER: Yes, Majesty. A succession of very old ships. Poorly maintained, yet richly insured.

ELIZABETH: Whose cargoes mysteriously vanished between safe harbour and the rocks.

FROBISHER: We are happy to inform Her Majesty that we sail on this occasion with the full support of the Admiralty.

ELIZABETH: Really. And?

FROBISHER: And provisions for our ships, we also require provisions.

ELIZABETH: Naturally. A voyage by England's most fearless sea-captain dare hardly go short of biscuits.

FROBISHER: Also, we need soldiers, Majesty, a militia to protect us from the savage.

ELIZABETH: Now you are being greedy. You may call yourself explorer, but we know you to be a sea-dog; a wolf may shed its coat, but its bite remains. You can still bite? Or have your teeth succumbed to the accursèd seal blubber?

FROBISHER: You may rely on my bite, Majesty, as ever. We thank Your Majesty. We will withdraw and await Her Majesty's pleasure…

ELIZABETH: You will withdraw when I give you leave.

So. We know what *you* discovered. What about Master Crowe. What did our physician find, when he split apart this 'Esquimaux'.

CROWE: I…I found everything in marvellous order, Your Majesty.

ELIZABETH: Not so marvellous it could keep him alive.

He had a heart, this Esquimaux?

CROWE: Yes, Your Majesty.

ELIZABETH: Organs? Liver, kidneys, pancreas?

CROWE: All exactly as your own, Your Majesty.

ELIZABETH: That I seriously doubt. What about the females? Is it true they have a horizontal cunt? I'm curious.

CROWE: I…I could not properly say, Your Majesty.

ELIZABETH: Pity. You're not *very* curious about humanity, are you, Master Crowe. My half of it.

FROBISHER: We think it unlikely, Majesty. The women, as with the men, *appear* very like ourself.

ELIZABETH: No doubt the women suffer. What about language. I suppose English is not spoken in your ill-named island?

FROBISHER: It's a babble, Majesty, not unlike the beasts.

ELIZABETH: That is a pity. I have a passion for languages of all kinds. And a heart for all peoples. All honest peoples.

CROWE: Their language is unintelligible to us, as yet, Your Majesty. You would find it, I'm sure, an intriguing system of sounds.

ELIZABETH: Do they grunt like the Bavarians? Or does their speech flow like the slippery French? Quelle belle journée pour se promener dans une tempête de neige.

FROBISHER: Very good, Majesty. C'est beau.

CROWE: N'importe quel jour est beau quand on se promene avec la reine.

ELIZABETH: Ah, votre français est bien délicat, Monsieur Crowe, ainsi que vos trés aimables sentiments.

CROWE: Malheuresement, j'ai appris ma plus part de mon français des livres, Majeste, mais les sentiments sont sincère.

FROBISHER: It's more like men from Cathay, Majesty; gibberish.

ELIZABETH: What appears gibberish to you, Captain, may be eloquence itself, to a scholar. Won't you agree, Master Crowe?

Beat.

CROWE: The Captain is a scholar of navigation, Your Majesty. It is only at court, he may appear to flounder.

FROBISHER: Master Crowe did learn some of their words, Majesty.

ELIZABETH: Oh?

CROWE gulps and thinks quickly.

CROWE: Indeed. The sound for fish, for example, is extraordinary. It sounds something like, erm, 'quwahl'.

ELIZABETH: Quwahl.

CROWE: Longer, Ma'am. Quwaahl.

ELIZABETH: Quwaahl.

CROWE: Yes. Bravo.

ELIZABETH: Walsingham. Quwaahl. Esquimaux. Meaning 'fish'.

WALSINGHAM: Yes, Ma'am.

FROBISHER: Though it may have been 'eat'. Or 'food'. We hope to discover more, Majesty. On our new voyage.

Beat.

ELIZABETH: What do these creatures eat? Do they take mutton, or pork?

FROBISHER: They grind bones and fishheads with their bare mouths, Majesty, they are quite the most savage savages ever encountered, much in need of English manners.

CROWE: … and yet, there is within the Esquimaux, much potential, Your Majesty. When shot and killed, a man's comrades weep for him, though in that frozen air, his tears turn to quickest crystal. And the women – I believe it is the women – do sing, most affectingly…

ELIZABETH: Sing? You heard this yourself?

FROBISHER: On our new voyage…(we hope to discover more)

ELIZABETH: Quiet. Master Crowe pray continue.

CROWE: One night, as we stood offshore, there was a good moon, some of the men and myself were on deck. Their voices came to us across the ice. The noise an angel might make, if we might hear the angels. A golden sound.

Beat.

ELIZABETH: I should like to hear an Esquimaux sing.

I charge you with a task, Master Crowe. Bring me an Esquimaux. I would like to meet one.

CROWE: Your Majesty…(I'm not sure that will be possible)

ELIZABETH: Alive, this time. And bring me his wife. I have questions for her. One who can sing.

FROBISHER: Master Crowe will take joy in accomplishing everything you ask, Majesty.

CROWE: I…I will indeed try to accomplish it, Your Majesty.

ELIZABETH: Do not try Master Crowe. We declared trying illegal this morning. You will succeed, for my sake. And for England's.

CROWE: Yes, Your Majesty.

FROBISHER: Then you are decided…? You will give us a ship?

Beat.

ELIZABETH: Eighty-twenty on all you find.

FROBISHER: Sixty-forty.

ELIZABETH: Seventy-five twenty-five and that is final.

FROBISHER: We…thank you for your generosity, Majesty.

ELIZABETH: They shall have my ship The Ayde, Wally.

Mind you bring this ship back in one piece. And Captain; I do not take kindly to being bargained with by a pirate. Redeem yourself; bring me gold, lots of it.

FROBISHER: I will, Majesty. You may bank on it.

ELIZABETH: I intend to. Now. You may leave.

FROBISHER and CROWE bow, and exit.

WALSINGHAM: Remarkable men, Majesty.

ELIZABETH: Ha! The poet and the pirate; two sides of a very dodgy coin. Frobisher's sharp enough to bring me some profit, no doubt. He is above all things a man of commerce.

WALSINGHAM: And yet, the 'treasury' of the ocean, can so oft prove treacherous, Ma'am. Surviving the arctic I agree is to the Captain's credit; a second voyage seems a giddy venture, if I might say so.

ELIZABETH: It may be it is a giddy venture, Wally, but I confess to feeling some giddiness this morning. (*Arch.*) Perhaps perchance I drew a hot fever a'bed last night. My blood was certainly raised for much of it.

WALSINGHAM: I…am sorry to hear it, Your Majesty.

ELIZABETH: You'd better bring me the Scottish Dukes. If they don't cool our ardour, nothing will.

WALSINGHAM: Yes, Ma'am.

She has picked up the blubber again, He thinks to exit, but lingers, clearing his throat.

ELIZABETH: Was there something else, Wally?

WALSINGHAM: Touching upon the contraction of night-fevers Ma'am. Was that my Lord the Earl of Essex, I saw leaving earlier?

Beat.

ELIZABETH: My dear Sir Francis, I do think you know it was.

Oh dear. I feel a lecture coming on.

My Lord Devereux is always welcome, Wally, he's my Master of the Horse.

WALSINGHAM: Yes, I heard that.

ELIZABETH: And I heard that.

WALSINGHAM: I was merely surprised to see my Lord of Essex attending Your Majesty. In the light of recent news.

ELIZABETH: What news?

WALSINGHAM: There is talk about Lord Devereux at court, Ma'am.

ELIZABETH: The knives are out for poor Robbie. Too tall in the saddle. To feeble at chess. If you listen to court gossip, Wally, you're the poorer for it, I'm surprised at you.

WALSINGHAM: I took the liberty of compiling a short report, based on the intelligence. Perhaps you would like me to read it.

ELIZABETH: No. I would not. As is well known, I take no pleasure in trifles.

WALSINGHAM: Then you would do well to read it yourself, Your Majesty. As you often say, a man who cannot read is merely ignorant. A man who will not read...

ELIZABETH: Yes, alright.

A beat. She takes it, scans it, grasps its content and hands it back.

As I said...

WALSINGHAM: Your Majesty...

ELIZABETH: I TAKE NO PLEASURE IN IT.

Pause.

If it makes you happy, check it. Twice. Three times. If the suspicion persists, I will exile my Lord Essex, in person, here, myself.

There. There's an end to it.

WALSINGHAM: Yes, Your Majesty.

ELIZABETH: Now. Bring me the Dukes of Argyle and Rothesay. That's if you have no further poison for my ears...

WALSINGHAM: No, Your Majesty...

ELIZABETH: And Wally?

WALSINGHAM: Yes, Ma'am?

ELIZABETH: Be assured of your facts in this. A stemmed fever may often lead to chills. I would not have you catch my chill for any price.

WALSINGHAM: I will be most cautious of my health, Your Majesty.

WALSINGHAM bows and exits.

Alone, ELIZABETH spins the globe. She stops it spinning, with an angry thump, and exits to her bedchamber.

Lights.

2

A HEART EXPOSED

The same chamber, as before. Night. A candle. The box of seal blubber.

ELIZABETH sits on a chair set upstage, by the window, gazing into a hand-held mirror. Without her red wig, she cuts a pathetic figure, as she studies her reflection.

WALSINGHAM enters, and bows.

ELIZABETH: Francis. What time is it?

WALSINGHAM: Past eleven, Ma'am. A clear night. And a starlit one. The heavens have never been so full of stars.

ELIZABETH: I've changed my mind about seal blubber. It's rather good. You must try some.

WALSINGHAM: I won't, thank you, Ma'am. Your Majesty…

ELIZABETH: I insist. Try it.

WALSINGHAM: I recall trying was outlawed this morning, Ma'am…

ELIZABETH: Take it.

A beat. WALSINGHAM takes a piece and puts it in his mouth.

Sticky. Almost so it clamps the jaws.

WALSINGHAM: Nnnnng.

ELIZABETH: Some might find that a disadvantage. If one spends time and money, as I have, perfecting one's smile, one wishes one's smile should be displayed constantly. Sealing the jaws works well, don't you find?

WALSINGHAM jaws are jammed into a smile.

WALSINGHAM: Nnnnng.

She smiles back. He breaks into a cough and manages to get the dratted stuff discretely from his mouth.

ELIZABETH: I trust you didn't spit that out.

WALSINGHAM: Not at all, Your Majesty. See?

He gulps in an exaggerated fashion.

Gone.

She puts the box aside.

Concerning our earlier conversation, Madam…

ELIZABETH: Damn Frobisher, and damn his blubber – I guess what concerns you. You've not troubled my bedtime before.

So, tell it.

Don't. No need.

You know this? Of a fact?

WALSINGHAM: Yes Ma'am, I believe I do. Beyond doubting.

ELIZABETH: Poor Wally, you don't know whether to strut or crumple. Despair at my misery or joy at Robbie's defeat.

He is here again, tonight, I take it.

WALSINGHAM: Just before the midnight bell, Ma'am, as is my Lordship's regular custom.

ELIZABETH: Well. You had better send him in.

WALSINGHAM bows, exits, and returns with DEVEREUX. DEVEREUX fills the space, bowing extravagantly and flinging aside his scarlet cloak with a flourish. He is very drunk.

DEVEREUX: Your Majesty, at your service. May I say, you look radiant tonight.

ELIZABETH: You may leave us, Wally.

WALSINGHAM: But Your Majesty…

ELIZABETH: Leave us.

Exit WALSINGHAM.

DEVEREUX: Do you play in the shadows, my Lady? Or do you hope your young flame lights you up all night?

ELIZABETH: My Lord Essex, you've been drinking.

DEVEREUX: A little. I and some of the other young bucks were out…drinking.

ELIZABETH: Do you drink to remember or to forget?

DEVEREUX: I don't recall.

ELIZABETH: Perhaps you remember where you lay your head this morning? Do you remember, perhaps, you lay your head between my thighs?

DEVEREUX: If my Lady says I did, it must be so.

ELIZABETH: Come come Master Devereux, let us not be coy. Were you not lying inside me, this morning. Did you and I not swear our love, touch limb upon limb and fear mere skin would not contain our passion?

DEVEREUX: If it pleases my Lady to remember our moments in such detail, I choose to believe de-tale is true.

ELIZABETH: That's a yes, is it?

DEVEREUX: If I recall, Majesty, it was a yes yes YES.

But ssssh I am sworn to secrecy.

ELIZABETH: Ah yes. Secrets. Walsingham hath received intelligence, concerning those.

DEVEREUX: Sir Francis Walsingham received intelligence? That is a secret.

ELIZABETH: He is no fool, my Lord. Nor am I. It is said… it is suggested in his report…that the Earl of Essex…hath taken himself a wife.

Not by my permission. Not with my blessing. Not me.

I told Sir Francis, of course his report is rubbish.

DEVEREUX: Rubbish – absolute. Complete gutter trash.

ELIZABETH: So the only question you need answer, my Lord, is whether it is false rubbish, or the other sort.

DEVEREUX: Your Majesty…Your Majesty knows I love only her…

ELIZABETH: TRUE OR FALSE!

DEVEREUX: False.

ELIZABETH: False?

DEVEREUX: False…except…I met a widow…

ELIZABETH: Damn you.

DEVEREUX: She is no picture, Majesty, I promise! She is old and ugly, and incredibly rich! You keep me so short of money and I…I need money. Madam ask yourself, what else but furtherance could a fellow possibly see in such a hag?

Beat.

That didn't sound right.

ELIZABETH: Pray, don't concern yourself my Lord. It wasn't Wally's report told me, not really.

DEVEREUX: No?

ELIZABETH: No, Robbie. I looked in here. The moment I looked in the glass, it spoke to me.

DEVEREUX: The glass…spoke to you, Majesty…?

ELIZABETH: Oh yes. See, you can see its mouth. Right here.

DEVEREUX steps forward to look in the mirror. Without warning, ELIZABETH smacks his face with it, tennis-style – quite a blow. Adjusting her position, she smashes his face to a backhand – a real belt. DEVEREUX collapses to the floor. The mirror has broken. ELIZABETH grabs a shard of glass.

Now, in God's name, I'll hurt you, you prick!

She grabs his waist band.

DEVEREUX: No no no!!

WALSINGHAM and OTHERS enter and prevent her attempted castration of him.

WALSINGHAM: Your Majesty please…!

They are pulled apart, ELIZABETH shrugs off her captors.

ELIZABETH: Get off me!

DEVEREUX: Majesty it's only a marriage.

ELIZABETH: Only a…only a marriage. Only the thing I would have given you.

Astonished pause.

WALSINGHAM: Is this true Your Majesty? You'd marry this… this thing? How often I've counselled you to provide an heir – with anyone! – but with this…?!

Now I see it. You love him.

ELIZABETH: Rubbish.

DEVEREUX: You never said, my Lady…

ELIZABETH: Of course I never said! You're supposed to notice!!

Get him away from me. Get him away!

WALSINGHAM: Come away my Lord…

DEVEREUX: No I won't…

WALSINGHAM: Yes, my Lord…

ELIZABETH: Take him to the Tower. Where people rot and die, and traitors lose their heads.

Oh yes my Lord I will have your head for this. See if I don't.

Treason!

Shocked pause.

WALSINGHAM: Your Majesty, you can't really mean…

ELIZABETH: Can't? Can't?!

(*To DEVEREUX.*) Oh, we know the answer to 'can't', don't we, my Lord. We have a maxim for it. 'Why not?'

DEVEREUX is dragged away. WALSINGHAM and ELIZABETH remain.

WALSINGHAM: Your Majesty…

ELIZABETH: Don't 'Your Majesty' me! Don't.

I shall be alone.

WALSINGHAM exits. A pause. Alone ELIZABETH staggers around a little, picking up bits of the mirror, then when they are all gathered, throwing them down again, she yells after WALSINGHAM.

I will not sit here and suffocate!

Breathing heavily, she stops, for breath, leaning against the globe. She loosens her collar, feeling her rising, feverish temperature – then passes out.

ELIZABETH's spirit exits through the open window.

We are carried into a raging storm; heaving sea, shouted orders of seamen desperately trying to save their ship. A huge groan of wood and ice – then silence, but for the wind, whistling across the tundra…

3

FRIESLAND

A pristine, empty, white space. Empty, except for the body of CROWE, a rope tied from his waist, and a bundle.

Enter FROBISHER gasping, crawling on his belly, clinging to the safety of the ice. He has a rope tied around his waist. When he reaches centre-stage he rolls onto his back, straining and gasping as he drags his bundle of belongings onto the ice. Then falls back, exhausted.

After a moment, FROBISHER *recovers enough to sit up.*

FROBISHER: Crowe.

> *He prods his partner with his booted foot, and again.*

> CROWE *is not stirring.* FROBISHER *knows what the cold can do. He gets to his feet, hurriedly cuts his bundle from his waist, and takes* CROWE *by the lapels.*

> Name. Name, Crowe!

CROWE: W-where are we?

FROBISHER: Name!

CROWE: C-Crowe. William Crowe.

FROBISHER: Get up. To your feet, man.

> FROBISHER *releases him, and staggers away, winded.* CROWE *slumps to the ground again.* FROBISHER *notices, walks back, and grabs him again.*

> Count.

CROWE: What?

FROBISHER: Count, Crowe!

CROWE: No no, plain…(Master William Crowe…)

FROBISHER: To ten, damn you. On yer feet.

> *He cuts* CROWE's *rope, drags him to his feet.*

> On yer feet. One two three… That's it. Walk. Four five six…

CROWE: Five six seven…

FROBISHER: …seven, good, keep going…eight…

CROWE: …eight, nine…eight…sev…

He's gone again, slumped to the ground.

FROBISHER: On yer feet Crowe. On yer feet!

A moment.

FROBISHER gives up.

Damn him. If a man begs for death, let him have it.

He takes out a pistol, points it at CROWE – the coup de grâce. He pulls the trigger – only water plops out. He throws the gun away, and talks to the living corpse.

Seven oceans. Seven oceans Crowe. Ice storms, leviathans…ice storms. Beasts…

His gaze is momentarily caught by the distant sea – or what might be in it. He drags himself back to the immediate concern.

Cold.

He places his hand on CROWE's forehead – to see if he is alive.

Cold as meat.

He looks about him.

Alone.

He continues to talk to CROWE – taking refuge in venting his grievances.

Esquimauxs'll come. Flesh-eating savage. Oh yes. Hunters, those boys – with spears, with knives. They'll hack you for supper. You won't rot. Oh no. Ten weeks, a year, I'll be home. England, a hero. Tarts, queuing round the block. You'll be here, exactly where you fell. William Crowe. Wiped from history.

You'll be sorry then. Weep, then. Saltwater melts ice. Warm currents'll melt your blood and one day – ping; you wake.

Too late, Crowe. Raped by mermaids. They'll make a man of you, those mermaids. Blond hair, breasts like pillows.

Bastard.

He kicks him again. No reaction. Again, he glances around. He's actually quite afraid – but defiant.

I am captain of a ship. An English fleet. I came to conquer for Elizabeth.

A decision. FROBISHER opens CROWE's bag and sorts through his gear.

Biscuits, damp. Edible.

Map… (*It has fallen to pieces.*)

Holy Water. (*Smells.*) Rum!

(*He drinks, smiles.*) Thank Christ.

He puts the flask down and returns to the bag. Unseen by FROBISHER, CROWE's hand flops out, reaching for and grabbing the flask. CROWE drains the flask, as FROBISHER continues his inventory.

Plate.

Beads, for trading…

Letter, from Her Majesty. 'To the Esquimaux it concerns'.

He laughs, kisses the letter, his mood swinging darkly with the next find.

Poison. The dying man's friend. Property of William Crowe, Physician. (*His eyes are dragged towards CROWE.*)

Meat.

He drags his gaze away from CROWE's corpse, pulls the stopper out of the poison phial, decides against that option. Puts it down in favour of the rum – which has miraculously returned to its place. CROWE meanwhile picks up the phial of poison, and quietly drains it.

More rum.

To life. Life in a land of dreams. A certain, lonely, conquering death.

FROBISHER lifts the flask to his lips… Nothing. He stares unbelieving at the empty flask, then around him.

Oh Unnatural Land…

Behind him CROWE chokes into life. He kneels on all fours spitting out the poison.

Alive, Crowe! Thank God! Crowe, yer alive!

CROWE: Dead. Poisoned!!!

FROBISHER: What the…?!!

CROWE: Fast – or slow? Fast or slow!

FROBISHER grabs the bottle, examines the label.

FROBISHER: Fast poison…! Oh Cruel Fate!

They wait for the poison to take effect. Nothing. FROBISHER, glances again at the bottle, then tosses it away.

Physician be damned! Thank God yer a humble surgeon. And I do love thee for it.

He kisses CROWE on the head.

Check the gear, stand up. Check the gear Crowe!

CROWE: You. I'll walk home.

FROBISHER: What? No. Stay together. I'll not lose you now Crowe.

CROWE: I can't breathe. Top of the world…

CROWE makes to leave, FROBISHER takes hold of him.

FROBISHER: You are a genius! Mmm? My genius. Other men lie cheat steal, persuade a man black is white white is black, grey is the colour of the sun.

CROWE looks at the sky.

CROWE: Grey…*is* (the colour of the sun)

FROBISHER: Not you, Crowe. You are the fool of kings. (*Reminding him.*) Mmm?

CROWE: That. That is a long time away…   England is very, very far away…

FROBISHER: One word, and you opened her treasury as wide as heaven. One word of brilliance!

CROWE: You mean, one word of perjury.

FROBISHER: Hear Oh Friesland the word of a genius!

Speak, William. Speak.

CROWE: Quwaaaahl.

FROBISHER: Louder.

CROWE: Quwaaahl.

FROBISHER: Louder!!

CROWE: Quwaaaahl!!

They laugh…FROBISHER repeating the word ad lib.

FROBISHER: Esquimaux. Meaning fish.

They laugh again – they are light-headed and hysterical, FROBISHER more so, so that CROWE is the first to sober, and his thoughts are dark.

CROWE: That creature, that Esquimaux you brought to me in Harwich. Dead a week. No words from him. I told you, I never did, never had, never wished to leave dry land – leave England – ever. Ever!

FROBISHER: You opened a world to her, Crowe! A kiddies book. (*He makes the gesture of a pop-up book.*) Bring me an Esquimaux! I navigate half across the globe. Search for a land no one has seen. Half the world doesn't believe in it! 'There goes Frobisher – he seeks a new world.' 'There be dragons, Frobisher.' (*He laughs again.*) I hit home. I hit home in Friesland!!

CROWE nods.

CROWE: Twice. Out there.

FROBISHER: That was unavoidable…

CROWE: All the world is splinters, screams of drowning men.

FROBISHER: You scare, too easy, Crowe. Ship's fine. Few boards lost, nothing more. Ship rides at anchor. See?

They do the 360-degree survey. Nothing.

CROWE: And the rowing boat. The rowing boat Frobisher?!

FROBISHER: Not the first to be sunk by a beast!

We hold on, you and me. We conquer, for Elizabeth and for us!

CROWE: What beast?

FROBISHER: Leave it.

CROWE: What beast?

FROBISHER: Walk.

CROWE: What beast did you see, Frobisher?

FROBISHER: Nothing. A shape, nothing more.

CROWE: What kind of shape? A bear, a giant – The Cyclops?!!!

FROBISHER: Passed over us. Beneath us. Port to starboard. Starboard to…how do I know what shape? Destiny, has made us live Crowe. Spared us for what works? Mmm? Think. For what works is any man born? For what purpose did the Maker make you? That we should come here – the genius, and the Gold-Finder General. To claim Friesland for the crown.

FROBISHER embraces CROWE, then makes to exit.

Walk, Master Crowe.

CROWE: Frobisher. I have spent a month. Sea-sick, morning to night. Guts thrown to the sea. Ice storms, rowing boat-wreck, poisons! Every night the last thought – is this soft sleep that comes, or death? – now this. Do you not think some god here wants us dead? Some hand of destruction hovers over us?

FROBISHER: Move on, Master Crowe. The rest'll find us soon enough…

CROWE: Rest? There's no one here! We are the only people in Friesland!

FROBISHER looks all around him.

FROBISHER: The whole of paradise. To ourselves.

CROWE: Paradise?

FROBISHER stoops to pick up a handful of snow.

FROBISHER: Feel, Crowe. White snow, on black earth, base rock wrapping pure gold. Gold, for Her Majesty. Or for us. Mmm? Seventy-five twenty-five? I say, seventy-five, seventy-five or nothing!

CROWE: You can't have seventy-five… What have you done?

FROBISHER: Nothing.

CROWE: Frobisher.

FROBISHER: A few extra ships. Unregistered vessels. More loads, different ports – you know how tight she is, it's a precaution, protect our investment. Mmm? I will make you rich Master Crowe. Then you can pay an Esquimaux to say 'quwaaaahl'. And sing. You can study medicine, be a proper man, become a genuine physician!

CROWE: A physician…

FROBISHER: Gold speaks all tongues Crowe, it says 'open sesame' in every one. Schools of medicine hear and obey like any whore.

CROWE: No longer a surgeon, with splattered books…

FROBISHER: You see? The land of dreams, Master Crowe. Friesland is the land of dreams!

CROWE: Frobisher, I have not said this. I have followed you, I will follow you over mountains, across deserts. For you are the greatest leader of men, ever known.

FROBISHER: Aye, William. And you are a great follower. Partner.

He kisses CROWE's head a second time, turns to exit, checks.

Wait.

Pulled up short by this new thought, he pads his pockets.

I had something. When I left England, I definitely…

CROWE: Bag.

41

FROBISHER: No.

CROWE: Gun?

FROBISHER: No.

CROWE: Crew.

FROBISHER: Yes. My crew…my handsome crew…

CROWE: All gone and drowned, Captain.

FROBISHER: But…but I had a Bo'sun, a portly man, old as time. Full of tales of the sea – he wore the brightest stockings in England!

Upstage, BO'SUN appears, followed by the rest of the CREW, unseen by FROBISHER.

And a midshipman, Mr Walker…whose mouth is foul as a trawlerman's, but a hardy sailor, and true…

MR WALKER: Fuck this Bo'sun, it's freezing here!

FROBISHER: …and a boy, a Ship's Boy, a young lad, but so eager to serve.

SHIP'S BOY: Here, Sir. You called Captain…?

FROBISHER: All lost you say?

CROWE: Lost in the deepest, bitterest ocean ever known to man.

FROBISHER: Did none survive…?

CROWE: None.

FROBISHER: Oh woe!

BO'SUN: Captain Frobisher?

Now FROBISHER sees them – or their likeness. He gasps.

FROBISHER: So now these apparitions…taunt our minds. Cruel elements toy with us! Isle of nightmares!

BO'SUN: No apparition Captain, your own men – true as we stand on the frozen earth.

FROBISHER: What – art real?

BO'SUN: Touch.

He holds out his hand. FROBISHER reaches out and touches, and a smile breaks on his lips.

FROBISHER: We live!

He embraces the BO'SUN.

MR WALKER: Still fucking cold…

FROBISHER: Lads, we survived!

All embrace, except CROWE.

A crew! A very proper crew! Look around you lads, did I not promise? Did I not deliver? All this for destiny to write our names upon!

Spade, Bo'sun.

BO'SUN: Cap'n?

FROBISHER: Spade man, for the sake of charity. A spade!

A spade is found. FROBISHER takes it, and hacks at the ice.

Now boys! We dig for glory!

The CREW fall to, and scrabble at the ice.

There it is boys!

MR WALKER: I see it!

He reaches down and finds a rock, which is passed to FROBISHER. He holds it up for all to see.

FROBISHER: So boys, now, are we ready for an adventure?

ALL: Aye Sir!

FROBISHER: Then who will be our sea?

BO'SUN: Me Cap'n.

FROBISHER: Alright! And are you right, Bo'sun? Your position fixed fair?

BO'SUN: I am Sir. Sun's to the east, thin ice that way.

'I am the roaring sea, devouring men
Spitting gold-drawn heroes, again.'

FROBISHER: Mr Walker – you'll be our Inlet I fancy. One way to glory, same way home.

MR WALKER: Aye Sir.

(*Performing simple actions.*) 'I am the icy inlet, that let us into Friesland…and out.'

FROBISHER: Boy.

SHIP'S BOY: Sir?

FROBISHER: That peak over there. If Bo'sun is the sea, where are you?

SHIP'S BOY: I am…here Captain.

FROBISHER: No no, further west. Master Crowe. What will you be?

CROWE: I will be…I will be whatever is needed. There are no trees here. What can I be. What's left? It is so cold here, and so bright…

FROBISHER: Cling on Master Crowe, this is a play for glory, remember?

CROWE: Then I am… I am the pedestal that rises from the ice. Over there! Or there…

FROBISHER: Oh, these pedestals come and go, Master Crowe.

CROWE: They go again?

FROBISHER: Season by season. Hour by hour.

MR WALKER: Like all the ice in the arctic…

BO'SUN: It fell from the stars they say. That's why it's bright, and cold.

CROWE: Then is nothing fixed, nothing?

BO'SUN: 'Tis a shifting place, they say. Risky, for warm-blooded men.

FROBISHER: But the rock remains. And here lies the prize, eh lads. Mr Crowe's prize as well as ours.

He lays it gently on the snow.

CROWE: Then I'll be…I'll be Time. Not over tall – that is, I'm not a Long Time. That Short Time fixed 'tween Frobisher and gold. Glory!

ALL: Hurrah!

FROBISHER: Very good Master Crowe. And here – here is the best of our drama, which any of us may play… Your Majesty, 'twas here, between the mountain and the inlet, the sea and sundry chalk-white bones, we found your own black earth, and in it, gold.

SHIP'S BOY: (*Picking up spade.*) I'll dig some more Cap'n – find more gold!

FROBISHER: Not now lad.

MR WALKER: Daft bugger.

FROBISHER: Bones to the east, high point west, sea behind; a day's walk to our artery of Black Earth. Two if we're gentle. But we are set fair, eh lads. This half-gold paves our way to riches!

He casually tosses the rock to CROWE.

Follow your captain lads, to gold, and adventure, and untold wealth.

ALL cheer, and set off upstage, FROBISHER shouting, to the earth.

We survived! I am Lord of everything we see!

FROBISHER exits upstage. CROWE calls after FROBISHER.

CROWE: Thank God she is not here to hear you say it.

FROBISHER has not heard. CROWE speaks to himself, handling the rock.

Gold. So here is Friesland, Isle of Dreams.

He touches his head where the blessing fell.

Partner. Thank God.

Lights down. Shrieking wind leads into….

4
A WATCHING PRESENCE

A blizzard.

It clears to reveal the face of ELIZABETH. With her eyes closed, her face is a field of snow.

Her eyes snap open. She is somewhere, somehow, awake, watching.

Blackout…

5
OF SAVAGES

Blizzard wind tails off, leaving the distant ring of hammers/picks struck in ragged unison.

Lights up on the 'camp'. There is less snow now, a patched carpet of snow, over grey rock/shingle.

Offstage, the ring of hammers continues.

SHIP'S BOY sits centre-stage on a stool. CROWE stands nearby, cleaning a jar with a cloth.

SHIP'S BOY: So, let's get this straight. You lived the whole of your life in one place, till you came here.

CROWE: That's right. Apart from a short time, when I stayed in Ipswich.

SHIP'S BOY: But you went back to Harwich to become a surgeon.

CROWE: I did. A butcher's shop became available. I diversified.

That's when I met Captain Frobisher. He brought me an Esquimaux. That poor creature's life was over, but mine had just begun.

SHIP'S BOY: So, you inhabited Harwich man and boy.

CROWE: Precisely.

SHIP'S BOY: There you are then, you and me are the same.

CROWE: You think so? Cough properly. Now spit.

The SHIP'S BOY spits into a cloth, which CROWE will examine.

SHIP'S BOY: I've lived in the same place all my life. Just, that place moves about a bit. Africa, the Indies. A ship moves on the swell too of course. A sailor is like a priest, he is constantly 'tween heaven and earth. Unless he's drowned…

The seas we had in the Indies, they were massive…all day, up and down, up and down…up and….

CROWE: (*Feeling the sickening swell.*) Yes, alright, thank you.

I'm going to give you some rags.

SHIP'S BOY: No brandy? Brandy's best Master Crowe.

CROWE: Brandy is in short supply. Rags are not. Here. When you cough, cough into these. Then bring them to me.

SHIP'S BOY: They won't let me leave the quarry every time I get a gobbit.

CROWE: Once a day will do. Bring me the cloths every other day at least. Until we sail.

SHIP'S BOY: That won't be long. Summers go quick here, eh Master Crowe.

He coughs – and passes over the rag.

Phlegm collecting. Ugggh. You should get out more.

CROWE: Coming to Friesland is 'getting out' quite enough, thank you.

SHIP'S BOY: True what they say then; you never even sailed before.

CROWE: Just because a man doesn't travel, doesn't mean he can't see the world, does it.

Beat.

SHIP'S BOY: I think it does Master Crowe…

CROWE: Nonsense. There are books, charts. What about them?

SHIP'S BOY: Books?

He breaks into a hacking cough.

CROWE: With a book you can travel anywhere. Explore other minds, other worlds. A man gets but one life on earth, but with books he can see any number of worlds – past, present – look through other men's eyes, compare one view with another, a hundred views.

More than any one man could, in one lifetime, no matter how many times he sails.

SHIP'S BOY: Not if you don't read Master Crowe. Books are no use to me. I'd be sat at home blind as a bat. Don't matter how many books you give me, I'd be marooned.

CROWE: I suppose so.

How many fingers?

SHIP'S BOY: All of them. Tell you don't work in the quarry. Frostbite takes a finger off everyone. Or a toe. Mr Walker thought he'd grown an extra toe. Turned out it wasn't his – he'd put the wrong boot on. That's Friesland for you.

CROWE: (*Inspecting cloth.*) There's a lot of dust in this. I'm not sure quarry work is good for you.

SHIP'S BOY: Like the tin miners say: 'Every lung has a silver lining.' I've got gold dust in my lungs Master Crowe.

CROWE: Not gold. Green phlegm mainly, and grit. We're lucky you survived this long. Another night like the last and you might not.

SHIP'S BOY: I'm just glad the Esquimauxs haven't got me. You ever meet an Esquimaux Master Crowe? A live one.

CROWE: Not yet. But I'm hopeful.

SHIP'S BOY: Hopeful?

CROWE: As you are for gold.

SHIP'S BOY: That's not a hope, that's a certainty. You ask the Captain. We must have tons of Black Earth now.

CROWE: As I said, there doesn't seem to be any…(gold) Well.

Enter BO'SUN, stage left, carrying a trunk.

BO'SUN: Morning Master Crowe. You keeping this boy from his work again?

CROWE: No, I'm doing my work as physician. Keeping the boy well enough to do his work. And from what I've seen, most of yours.

BO'SUN: Physician he says. Is that pork physician or beef?

Enter MR WALKER, his face blackened with soot.

CROWE: How is it going Mr Walker? You've stopped the hammering.

BO'SUN: Time we had a rest, got warmed up a bit. The boy can take a turn.

CROWE: Mister Bo'sun I've no desire to argue…

BO'SUN: Good.

CROWE: You know, if you wish to stay warm we should play some games.

MR WALKER: Games? No time for games here. Barely time to eat, that right Bo'sun.

BO'SUN: That's right.

MR WALKER: Nothing to bloody eat when we do have time.

CROWE: Well then, we must make your work a game.

BO'SUN: Better you leave the work to us Master Crowe. Men who are used to it. Eh lads.

CROWE: I insist. I may not be an actual physician, but I know about this.

This trunk is empty is it?

BO'SUN: Is now.

CROWE: And those rocks over there need packing in it.

MR WALKER: He's got the hang of the theory then.

CROWE: And normally you'd take the trunk over there, and fill it from the quarry.

BO'SUN: That's the boy's work. When he's left to it.

The SHIP'S BOY can't prevent a coughing fit.

CROWE: Well, I say we keep the trunk here, and throw the rocks from the quarry across to it. That way we load the Black Earth and stay warm. Like this.

(*Calling off.*) Over here!

A rock is thrown from the wing, caught by CROWE.

You see. To you Bo'sun…and now on to Mr Walker.

BO'SUN: Mr Walker.

MR WALKER: Boy.

CROWE: Back to me…

SHIP'S BOY: Master Crowe.

CROWE: …and I put it in the trunk. Like that.

SHIP'S BOY coughs again.

BO'SUN: That'll make us healthy will it.

CROWE: It'll help us keep warm, yes. Well?

BO'SUN: I reckon we could do that lads. Get Master Crowe's blood up for him.

BO'SUN whistles. A rock flies on, and is thrown with great pace and dexterity between the SAILORS, finally being dropped short for CROWE, who nonetheless, and with some triumph, manages to catch it.

CROWE: Good!

BO'SUN: In the chest then, Master Crowe.

CROWE: There you see – teamwork. Friesland could be good for us yet.

As he puts the rock in the chest, MR WALKER kicks down the lid, narrowly missing CROWE's fingers.

MR WALKER: Sorry, Master Crowe.

BO'SUN: This time then, lads.

He whistles again. A rock flies on from the wing and again is passed at great speed, this time everyone calling out CROWE's name but throwing it to someone else. It's like a playground game, with CROWE as piggy in the middle. By the time he catches it, it is with an exhausted dive to the ground. Suddenly, all the crew have rocks in their hands; when CROWE looks up, he realises he is at their mercy.

Steady now lads; scare the sow, the meat goes tough.

Off, a bell sounds.

CROWE: W-what? L-lads why don't you…(put the rocks down…)

BO'SUN: You got lucky, Master Crowe. Rum break.

They chuck the rocks down – a series of thuds. The moment has passed.

Alright. Gather round boys. Keep it quiet.

BO'SUN takes out a bag of food scraps and looted flasks from a secret place, and tips it out. All scrabble for a crust, or a drink…

Each retires to a space to chew on what they've managed to grab. Apart from CROWE, who isn't offered any.

CROWE: Ah, you have food too. Good.

Spirits are quickly restored by the food, which they continue to eat.

Well, I should probably…(be going)

MR WALKER: Here's one for you then Master Crowe. 'Fore you go back to your studies. Why do Esquimauxs have slitty eyes?

BO'SUN and SHIP'S BOY snigger.

CROWE: Ah, well, that's easy. The light here in the Arctic is very bright, when it strikes the snow it can be dazzling. In order to avoid being blinded…

SHIP'S BOY: You haven't really got the hang of this joke business, have you Master Crowe.

CROWE: Perhaps not. I'm not sure I really see the point.

MR WALKER: Can't see the point? In jokes?! That is the point!

CROWE: Jokes about Esquimauxs.

SHIP'S BOY: There's got to be jokes, Master Crowe! And the savage must learn the English to get the jokes. He won't know who's boss otherwise, ain't that right Bo'sun…

BO'SUN: Very well put, lad.

CROWE: Well we don't actually know that, do we. That they are 'savages'. We haven't met any Esquimauxs. At least I haven't. Not in Friesland.

SHIP'S BOY: Too right. I'm not talking to no savage.

MR WALKER: How do we know they're not bleeding cannonballs?? Eh, Master Crowe? Answer me that.

CROWE: Well…I suppose we don't know.

BO'SUN: They stay away from us, we stay away from them.

MR WALKER: One thing's certain, they don't all sing.

BO'SUN: Or say quwaahl!

All laugh at CROWE's expense.

CROWE: I just think we shouldn't jump to conclusions. If we could meet these people, we might learn from them. And they from us…

SHIP'S BOY: Learn from a savage?!

BO'SUN: Boy's right, Master Crowe. Be like the Americas, when they come for us. They use the voodoo to hunt – silent, deadly, creep across the ice, murder a man in his cot with an icicle, screwed deep in his heart.

MR WALKER: You won't scare Mr Crowe none, Bo'sun, I heard he cut one of they Esquimauxs up himself.

CROWE: Yes, well that was in England.

BO'SUN: Good for you Master Crowe.

CROWE: (*Indignant.*) He was already dead.

MR WALKER: Damn right Master Crowe. Can't be too careful.

CROWE: I wished to find out why my fellow human died. As soon as he reached England's shores.

MR WALKER: Fellow human?!

BO'SUN: Steady now, Mr Walker. Master Crow'll call you a savage, you go to argue with him.

SHIP'S BOY: (*Coughing.*)

CROWE: It's just…I'm not sure why we fear them so much.

SHIP'S BOY: (*Coughing.*)

MR WALKER: I don't fear 'em. Shoot on sight, that's my motto.

SHIP'S BOY: (*Coughing.*)

CROWE: Use a rag!

SHIP'S BOY: Yes Master Crowe.

> *He coughs into the cloth, and hands it back to CROWE.*

> Here's one for you then. Two Esquimauxs walking along the road. One says to the other…

BO'SUN / MR WALKER: 'That's an improvement.'

FROBISHER: (*Entering.*) Have you no work, lads.

> *FROBISHER carries a bucket. The CREW stuff food away, quickly. BO'SUN covers.*

BO'SUN: Yes Captain. Just loading this here trunk. Only Master Crowe kept us talking with his views on how all Esquimauxs is gentlemen.

> *MR WALKER marks on the trunk with chalk, and closes the lid.*

MR WALKER: One thousand three hundred and two. Ready for shipping.

FROBISHER: Bo'sun. Take the lads back. Load one thousand three hundred and three.

BO'SUN: You heard the Captain.

FROBISHER: And Bo'sun. Empty your pockets before you go.
All of you.

BO'SUN: Now, Captain…

FROBISHER tosses a padlock onto the ground.

FROBISHER: You are trusted with the key to the food store
Bo'sun. Empty yer pockets. Now.

*Beat. They all turn out bits of food, including at least one from
under a hat.*

Boy.

*SHIP'S BOY pulls a string and his trousers shower the snow with
lumps of black rock.*

SHIP'S BOY: I thought I could buy some food. When we got
home. Gold's no use to us here Captain.

FROBISHER: The penalty for thieving in my crew is flogging.
If you eat the food now, you'll starve later. Off you go.

BO'SUN: Chill's biting hard, Captain. I say, take what we
have and sail home now, 'fore winter sets in. The lads are
hungry, Captain…

FROBISHER: Then they must *be* hungry. We will sit out the
winter in Friesland.

Beat.

MR WALKER: We can't last out the whole winter…

FROBISHER: There is no choice. *You* froze over.

If we're tough, and determined and think of the prize, we'll
survive. As I always tell you.

MR WALKER: That's right. As you always tell us.

FROBISHER: Do you challenge me, Walker?

Beat.

BO'SUN: You heard the Captain lads. Back to work.

They troop off. FROBISHER empties his bucket on the ice – ashes that fizzle out in the snow.

CROWE: No gold from the rock again.

Beat.

(*Very chirpy.*) Is everything else well?

Beat.

Frobisher, it's only a matter of time, I'm sure before…

FROBISHER: Before we starve to death.

Enough of that.

I've a job for you Master Crowe. Job for an expert.

CROWE: I shall do what I can, Captain. Though I'm no expert in fire-setting. If you need hotter fires…

FROBISHER: Your beloved Esquimaux; they're out there. Watching. I can feel it.

CROWE: (*Excited.*) You want me to lead a party, make a treaty with them?

FROBISHER: There'll be no treaties. I found a man dead this morning, on the ice. Savaged.

CROWE: One of our men?

FROBISHER: No. Not one I've met. But an Englishman, that's beyond doubt.

CROWE: A stowaway? You're sure he's not an Esquimaux…?!

FROBISHER: Neither. He's a gentleman. A nobleman by the look of him. Dressed like a canary. Except…

CROWE: Except?

FROBISHER: Except he has no head.

CROWE: A bear. A beast? The beast you saw when we landed…! A head-eating monster, stalking the ice, killing without mercy…?!!

FROBISHER: It is the savages who kill in Friesland Master Crowe.

I'll double the guard tonight, we'll shoot on sight.

CROWE: Frobisher…

FROBISHER: Do not argue with my orders.

CROWE: What happened to exploration. Have you forgot that I have a royal commission for which my life is ransom. To fail Her Majesty…

FROBISHER: Finding an Esquimaux that sings. What song would you teach the savage, Master Crowe, if he were here now?

CROWE: I would teach him nothing. I hope I'd learn one of his songs.

FROBISHER: You'll need to teach an English song, for Her Majesty. Or a French one. Convince her they're civilised.

Sing for me now, Crowe. Anything.

CROWE: I…I only know sailor's songs. I hear them sometimes, below decks. They're not all bad, the men, it's just, with the dreams you give them, and privations of this place…

FROBISHER: Sing, Crowe. For pity's sake.

Beat. CROWE sings – a lilting lament.

CROWE: Once I had a true love
    and she was my Lady;
    and never did a lady
    wear so sweet a smile.
    And the eyes of my true love
    are the blue skies of the morning,
    the sun on English meadows
    mile on mile.
    Singing hey-ho, love
    Singing hey-ho, love
    Singing hey-ho, love
    Sing love.

    Soon I left my true love
    to sail upon the ocean;
    the deep swell of the ocean
    was my pillow for a while.
    And the dark of our darkest day,
    the terrors of the night-time,
    are shadows that pass swiftly
    across her eye.
    Singing hey-ho, love
    Singing hey-ho, love
    Singing hey-ho, love
    Sing love.

Beat. FROBISHER gets up with fresh determination.

FROBISHER: You'll take this corpse away, Master Crowe. Scoop him out, pack him with ice, preserve this noble Lord. Her Majesty'll be glad to have a kinsman returned in such fine order. She may even raid her collection to find a head that fits. Then perhaps she will overlook your failed commission. And mine, if it comes to that.

CROWE: Frobisher, I'm a surgeon, not an embalmer! Why do you only bring me corpses?

But I will do what you ask.

I will need my books. My anatomy…

FROBISHER: Then have it. Though the pages rot.

CROWE: Frobisher may I ask. Before, when we sailed…

FROBISHER: I am Commander of this expedition.

CROWE: You called us partners. What changed? I find no friendship in your tone. Let alone, affection.

FROBISHER: Affection. With you, Black Earth has gold one minute, none the next. I say savage; you say human. I say be tough, fight the elements, survive; you talk about treaties, being friendly, you dwell upon the men's sickness.

CROWE: I am a surgeon…!

FROBISHER: A man's will evaporates here. Freezes in mid-breath. In this world a man must be stone, or die. What's weak and soft is finished. That's why I am decided; from now on, you must be kept away from the crew. And they from you.

I'll send the corpse over.

MR WALKER: No need Captain. Package for you Master Crowe.

Enter SHIP'S BOY, dragging or pushing a sled bearing a long, roughwood box.

CROWE: Thank you boy. Do you have a name, boy?

SHIP'S BOY: Yes Sir. Boy. (*Coughs, apologises to FROBISHER.*) Sorry Sir.

He hands his rag over to CROWE.

Master Crowe's collecting them. Like you said Master Crowe, there's a lot of dust in there, still no gold.

CROWE: Thank you.

FROBISHER: (*To SHIP'S BOY.*) Back to work.

SHIP'S BOY exits. FROBISHER hands over a pistol.

(*To CROWE.*) Fire if you're attacked. Or take your chance with the savage, Master Crowe. Perhaps we will meet again. I hope so.

FROBISHER exits. Alone, CROWE touches the box, and addresses the occupant.

CROWE: No head, he says. What did you do, my Lord, to earn such a fate. Fell foul of some unyielding power. And him, my Captain – who changed the shape of the world. How far did he fall, when at last we came to earth.

Well. This is a strange land.

Come my Lord. We will travel together; me with my too many brains, and yours so cruelly dashed. Out into the cold, where lurks who-knows-what-a beast. Or beasts.

Hold fast, my Lord.

He pushes the sledge, and with it, exits…

Lights. Again, the wind whistles across the tundra.

6
THE ICE QUEEN

Another part of the island – a field of snow like the one CROWE has just left, only more desolate, with just a small block of ice downstage centre.

ELIZABETH: (*Offstage.*) You may rest here Wally.

WALSINGHAM: (*Offstage.*) You are very gracious, Majesty.

WALSINGHAM enters in a full-length fur coat, dragging a heavy sled full of cases and trunks, by means of a strap around his forehead.

He slips the strap off his head, and flops onto the block, exhausted and squinting.

ELIZABETH appears – she is dressed in a green velvet riding-dress trimmed with fur, gloves, her make-up much lighter. She also carries a small case, which she places prominently, downstage, while they rest.

ELIZABETH: Do not sit long on the ice. You will never satisfy the itch.

He offers to give up the seat.

WALSINGHAM: Please…

ELIZABETH: No no. I don't need to rest. I may have the heart and kidneys of a woman, but I am known for the constitution of an ox.

She looks around.

It is magnificent, is it not?

WALSINGHAM: Indeed it is, Majesty. The light, the air, the ground a carpet of diamonds, every step a satisfying crunch of boot on fresh snow.

ELIZABETH: Captain Frobisher is a gem of an explorer, did I not say it.

WALSINGHAM: Your words exactly, Majesty.

And I agree. His new land is almost perfection.

ELIZABETH: Almost perfection?

WALSINGHAM: It is rather chilly.

A terrifying creak in the ice.

What was that?

ELIZABETH: What was what?

A terrifying creak in the ice.

WALSINGHAM: That.

ELIZABETH: I hear nothing. Shall we take some food Wally?

A terrifying creak in the ice.

WALSINGHAM: Again.

ELIZABETH: Ah. That will be the ice beneath us. The ice in the Arctic is apt to split apart without warning, I believe. Or come together with a shudder.

Or it may have been the ship.

WALSINGHAM: Ship, Your Majesty?

ELIZABETH: You will not forget the ship I gave to Captain Frobisher. Over there. Nine score tons, square-rigged, quite ruined. I have heard a ship can be destroyed by force of ice alone in these parts. Not that Feckless Frobisher needs assistance. Or else lifted high in the air, to hang there on a pedestal.

ELIZABETH: We must find his crew, and give the men our blessing. I fancy they may need it.

WALSINGHAM: Perhaps Majesty we might light a fire first, warm ourselves with rugs and perhaps a beverage…

ELIZABETH: Come, Sir Francis. We have worse than this in England. Besides, I must also meet the Esquimaux, and Master Crowe has promised I shall hear them sing.

WALSINGHAM: But…but Your Majesty…you heard the pirate say it – the Esquimaux is a savage, flesh-eating creature, and there are bears in the land, unspeakable torments lurk around every…pedestal. To wander here in person is the utmost folly.

ELIZABETH: Quiet.

There, you see? Nothing.

Another creak.

We've had that one, it's an echo.

WALSINGHAM: But Majesty…

ELIZABETH: 'The new world and the old. Old England, New Empire. God's chosen, embracing the future.' An era of great conquest is upon us Wally. Do you wish to be part of the new era, or no?

WALSINGHAM: Of course, Your Majesty, but…

ELIZABETH: Good. Then we must put our best boot forward…

WALSINGHAM: Majesty, please…let us rest a little longer. Please?

Beat.

ELIZABETH: How long have you served me, Francis?

WALSINGHAM: More than a half a lifetime my Lady. Though it seems but a breath…

ELIZABETH: And you have served our country well, in that time?

WALSINGHAM: I do hope so, Your Majesty.

ELIZABETH: Then I shall make you a promise. Help me in this venture, and I will release you from your service.

WALSINGHAM: Release…but Your Majesty – Your Majesty knows I live only to serve the crown. There's not a day I don't wake with a mind bursting with schemes and ambition for Her Majesty, for England's advantage. I know I am old, but Majesty…

ELIZABETH: Alright, I'll keep you on. But you will promise me one thing.

WALSINGHAM: Anything, my Lady.

ELIZABETH: Stop saying 'But Majesty…' it grates.

WALSINGHAM: But Maj…

ELIZABETH: There. It aggravates. I have not said this before. Your voice reminds me each morning of a child with skates.

WALSINGHAM: With skates, Your Majesty…?

ELIZABETH: Skating on the inside of the skull. The child falls over, gets up, skates a while longer, falls over, and begins to scream in such a way as a child does scream.

Ow ow! Help! My ankle! My ankle, oh, it is broke!

Help me mother, help!

There, I've said it.

WALSINGHAM: Forgive me Your Majesty. I shall endeavour to be less…less like a child on skates, in future.

ELIZABETH: What a freedom we find here to say exactly what we think. Are we rested?

WALSINGHAM: No Your Majesty. Yes Your Majesty. Though if I might say so…

ELIZABETH: (*Warning.*) Wally…

WALSINGHAM: I mean merely to speak to Your Majesty a well known saying. If one wishes to embrace the future, one has only to wait. The future comes to us.

ELIZABETH: That, Sir Francis, is a recipe for sloth. Dare I say it, underachievement. You are butting, whether you say the word or no. England will be great, or she will be nothing. I plump for greatness. There is nothing else.

There. I've said that too.

Bring the luggage.

Not that one. That one stays with me. That is my burden, Wally. A thing I have taken for myself; I shall dispose of it as I choose.

She picks up the bag, holding, with a tenderness her sternness can't quite hide.

WALSINGHAM: Your Majesty I'm inclined to believe the contents of that bag is a most grave encumberance to you, perhaps my Lady I might…

ELIZABETH: Nonsense. I don't give a fig for its contents. We'll press on.

Wally?

Exit ELIZABETH.

WALSINGHAM: Oh this land of stars.
That small Island of sweetness.

(*He casts a glance after ELIZABETH.*)

That such pain should lie beneath her royal, frozen crust.

ELIZABETH: (*Off.*) Wally!

WALSINGHAM: (*Calling.*) But of course my Lady…

(*Privately.*) Not pain, obviously, but the purest gold.

(*Calling.*) …coming, Your Majesty…

He has heaved himself to his feet, and now takes up the reigns again, pulls down the googles, and pulls the sled, slowly, a great weight...

I really do think Your Majesty, next time we pursue a new empire, we might find one a little more clement. One that does not bite the fingers, and tear at the cheeks so. And does not have polar bears, or...pedestals...or ice that creaks.

The ice creaks – bang on cue. He jumps at it.

ELIZABETH: (*Off.*) Onward, Wally.

Exit WALSINGHAM, and the sled, as the wind whistles across the tundra. Lights.

7

WILDERNESS

CROWE approaches across the ice, exhausted, pulling the sled with its ominous trunk. He stops, opens the lid, and discovers a scarlet robe.

Lights.

End of Part One.

Part Two

8
OF HEADS AND HEARTS

The same. DEVEREUX's corpse is hidden from our view by the scarlet blanket, now folded back, only the feet showing; the body is visible to those who stand over him, but not to us.

A fire crackles nearby.

Enter CROWE, his sleeves rolled up. With a bucket he tips some driftwood onto the fire. He puts the bucket down. He speaks to the corpse on the slab.

CROWE: How are we, my Lord. Are we thawed yet?

I forgot. You have no head. What else can you not declare?

He takes a scalpel and pokes it in the stomach cavity, identifying the parts.

Liver, kidneys, pancreas. All exactly as our own.

You will not need them here my Lord. These vitals make you soft. Heart… Where is the heart… Hearts…?

Praise God in heaven – two hearts?!

What unnatural place is this?

A great groaning, crack of ice.

Enter ELIZABETH, as ever, carrying her bag.

ELIZABETH: Praise God indeed, Master Crowe…

I knew it. You're a priest.

CROWE: Your Majesty!

ELIZABETH: I know we meet in a strange land, Master Crowe. I trust manners are not completely foreign here.

CROWE remembers, belatedly, to drop to his knee and bow his head.

CROWE: Forgive me Majesty. I was confused, I believed I was alone.

ELIZABETH: That is a feeling I know well.

CROWE begins to rise.

Stay!

I have a bone to pick with you, Master Crowe. Though I see you have begun without me…

CROWE: (*Starting to rise.*) Majesty…

ELIZABETH: Stay! I spotted a number of Esquimaux on my journey here. Seen from a distance, across the snow, the natives of this land are round people – thimbles viewed across a tablecloth. Being of a limited vocabulary in their tongue, and they ignorant of mine, I was not able to request them to sing. But I was able to call out one word. The one word I had been vouched-safe was theirs.

Quwaaahl.

Quwaaahl quwaaaahl, I cried.

Then with a new emphasis, in case the mistake was mine:

Quwa-aahl, quwa-aahl.

CROWE: Majesty, if I may explain…

ELIZABETH: No Sir, you may not. I, on the other hand, am well placed to interpret. Either 'spear' 'rock' and 'snowball' are synonyms for the word 'fish' – or we have been royally misled. At considerable danger to the royal person. If the word 'quwaaahl' is indeed a fish, it is evidently a red herring.

CROWE: Majesty…I believe there are a number of dialects among the natives… Perhaps my information was… optimistic in its considered…universality of application.

ELIZABETH: You may rise, Master Crowe. I shall thank you to be as full in your research as you are fat in vocabulary.

CROWE: Yes Majesty, I will. You must forgive me, Your Majesty, you gave me quite a shock.

ELIZABETH: On the contrary Master Crowe. I gave you a ship. You and that partner of yours – the feckless and invisible Frobisher. A ship I bartered for a live version of what we see before us. You have no luck with the Esquimaux *in situ* I see.

CROWE: No Majesty. That is, this is not an Esquimaux. As such.

ELIZABETH: Come come Master Crowe, one cannot be an Esquimaux as such. One is either an Esquimaux, or one is not.

CROWE: He is an Englishman, Ma'am.

ELIZABETH: *Ipso facto* he is not an Esquimaux.

CROWE: No Majesty. Though in a better age I hope an Esquimaux might be welcomed as an Englishman. And… vice versa…perhaps…

Beat.

ELIZABETH: I'm surprised a physician as notable as yourself cannot get corpses at home.

CROWE: (*A desperate change of subject.*) You are alone, Majesty?

ELIZABETH: No indeed. Sir Francis Walsingham is with us – but complains of toothache. Among every other ailment. I sent him to find food.

The man you are investigating is a casualty of the expedition, I take it.

CROWE: Yes, Majesty. Though not a casualty of our making.

ELIZABETH: Natural causes. That must be dreary for a physician.

CROWE: On the contrary Majesty. This man is a scientific phenomenon. And I am not, in fact, a physician Your Majesty. I am but a surgeon, a self-taught hewer of men.

ELIZABETH: Whatever you are, you've made a fair stab at it. Let me see.

CROWE: Majesty, I think, you should not look, just yet.

ELIZABETH: You needn't worry for me, Master Crowe. I have attended a number of anatomical surveys. I may have the body of a weak and feeble woman, but I have the nose and stomach of a vulture. I am not a person given to the vapours, I can assure you.

CROWE: This body has been cruelly treated, Majesty. Disfigured, quite terribly. And unusual in a number of respects. Lacking in some things and doubly equipped in others…

ELIZABETH: That is true of many men. A little blood does not trouble a queen of England, we are famed for it. Stand aside.

CROWE does so – reluctantly obeying an order. ELIZABETH moves so she can see, slowly walks around the corpse, takes it all in, turns to CROWE, smiles – and passes out. CROWE catches her.

CROWE: Majesty!

(*Calling.*) Hello? Help there?

No response. CROWE has to manage by himself. He drags her round to the block, stage right, where she can sit to recover herself.

Majesty, rest awhile. Forgive me, I should not have let you look.

ELIZABETH: What? Forgive me Master Crowe. I did not faint.

I merely thought, for a moment, I knew the man.

CROWE: Perhaps he is a relative, Your Majesty?

ELIZABETH: Relative, no. Though it's true we may have shared relations. I did think, for a moment, he was familiar to me. And this scarlet… How came you by this body Master Crowe?

CROWE: He was found dashed upon the ice. Cast out from human company, and parted from his head.

It is unusual to recognise a man without his face.

ELIZABETH: That's true. The man I knew had a most pleasant face.

And a good leg. And a happy manner. And a glint in the eye that made me laugh. A touch on warm skin that could bring a gentle balm. I'm settled. Help me see him again.

CROWE: But Your Majesty…

ELIZABETH: Don't 'but', Master Crowe. Help me.

Again she surveys the body.

Yes. It was the lack of a head I noticed first. And then the rest, that too seems all…familiar.

CROWE: He is as I said, a phenomenon, Your Majesty.

ELIZABETH: Nonsense. There are a dozen men like him, a hundred. Men are many to the penny, as nurse told me a dozen times….

CROWE: I have anatomised a dozen men or more myself, but this man has twice the endowment of any man I've seen.

ELIZABETH: Certainly he was an able man, I had no complaints there.

CROWE: The heart Madam.

This is not where she is looking…

ELIZABETH: What?

CROWE: I noticed first when I pushed the lung aside. He has, remarkably, two hearts. Kidneys, liver, pancreas, all are the same. But in the chamber here – you see? – beside his heart, his own, strong and fleshy valve, breeds another heart. A strong but frozen thing. The wonder is, the rest of him was all but thawed, but this – this stays cold, and chills the rest.

(*He reaches inside and holds it up.*) Do you see?

Again she swoons, but this time catches herself.

ELIZABETH: It's alright. I'm fine.

What a scabrous thing it has become, now I see it. This heart.

CROWE: You are…familiar with this heart?

ELIZABETH: I never saw it until this day – and yet I know it as my own.

Strange. The man who kept it told me once, I held his heart in the palm of my hand. Some people have a heart like soap. Don't you find, Master Crowe?

CROWE: I do, Majesty.

ELIZABETH: The hardest held, the soonest lost.

I should have told poor Robbie what he was to me. My heart might not have grown so cold against him.

Thank goodness we have our expedition. We'll take our gold from this haunted place and Elizabeth will make her mark. England will prosper, however much we're hurt. Whatever pain we harbour, England will be a second Spain.

CROWE: I think you won't, Your Majesty. Take gold from Friesland.

ELIZABETH: You are not telling me Master Frobisher has not found his Black Earth?

CROWE: He has, Majesty, found much Black Earth. I think a hundred tons and more, besides the rock he puts aside. And he will come again, on further journeys, with extra ships. He'll fetch more and more Black Earth, but not a speck of gold is there, however hot the fire gets. It's dross. All dross and broken men and ruined lives. There, now I have said it.

ELIZABETH: You know this, for a fact?

CROWE: I believe I do, Your Majesty.

ELIZABETH: You outshine the prophets, Master Crowe; I did not take you for a reader of entrails. No gold at all you say?

CROWE: None, Your Majesty. The rock – and there is much – is barren: good only for roads perhaps, or a wall.

ELIZABETH: Well. Thank God we have your Esquimaux, Master Crowe. You shall certainly bring me those. A new world needs new subjects, you bring me singing Esquimaux, and we will be satisfied. We shall learn their

ancient lore together Master Crowe, and Wally will press
England's ancient laws on them.

CROWE: I will try to bring them, Majesty, but I will not
succeed.

ELIZABETH: I made trying illegal. Underachievement.

CROWE: Majesty, I will bring a whole family of Esquimauxs –
men women and children, but all will come to naught. The
Green Fever, that some people call a cold, has become my
study here. The fever clings to us, but kills the Esquimaux.
I will try to bring my Esquimaux to you, but they will die
before they reach the goal.

ELIZABETH: You mean, before they reach the condition of
Civility?

CROWE: Before they reach the palace.

ELIZABETH: I hope you are not suggesting the savage get their
disease from us?!

CROWE: No, no, Majesty.

Except…we trespass here. And their defence is weak.
Arrows, snowballs, against our guns. The same is true of
sickness. Their land is cold, but it is we who make it bitter.
That is my belief.

ELIZABETH: (*Computing.*) They will not come near us here.
And die when they reach us in England. What you are
saying Master Crowe is, I shall never hear the Esquimaux
sing.

Do you have more bad news to impart? If you're a
surgeon, we may as well lance the boil.

CROWE: Only, Majesty – no, it is not my place.

ELIZABETH: Speak.

CROWE: This man it appears, has lost his head. If Your Majesty knows the whereabouts of such a treasure, perhaps we might proceed in the English way.

ELIZABETH: The English way?

CROWE: A trade, Your Majesty. Vouchsafe this man his head, and perhaps you may unfreeze your heart.

ELIZABETH: You speak very boldly Master Crowe – of your heads and hearts. And very rudely too. I hope you do not presume to know what's in every woman's handbag….

Beat.

CROWE: A queen who mixes mercy with her might
will make the best, less brittle steel.
It is not weak to shun the taking of a head,
so the heart can feel.

ELIZABETH: You rhyme very badly, too. Perhaps I should make you a judge, I've never heard so poor a sentence.

CROWE: Your Majesty, this man has fallen from the stars.

We too, know what it is to fall. And to see hope dashed.

Beat.

ELIZABETH: Poor Devereux. I do not want to take his head.

I cannot bear for him to live and not be mine. Unfolding words inside another's ear. To brush his lips across another's cheek.

Neither can I bear to never hear his voice again.

With great feeling and solemnity, she goes to fetch the bag. She places her hand upon the handle to pick it up. The front of the bag flops open. DEVEREUX's head grabs its chance.

DEVEREUX: Mercy Majesty, mercy!!!

She slaps the bag shut, silencing him.

ELIZABETH: Not the best of sounds.

CROWE: A trade, Ma'am?

She picks the bag up and is about to pass it over when…

FROBISHER: (*Off.*) Ho there! Now I spy the beast!

FROBISHER enters, musket at his eye, levelled apparently at the QUEEN and CROWE. MR WALKER, the SHIP'S BOY and the BO'SUN follow with swords.

I have the beast now! Down with you Crowe!!

CROWE ducks, FROBISHER fires the musket. He has missed.

Bastard!!

He throws down the musket in disgust.

CROWE draws attention to the royal presence…

CROWE: Captain Frobisher – Her Majesty The Queen is here.

FROBISHER: Aye.

He does a double take, yelps with terror, and leaps in the air, to be caught in the arms of the BO'SUN.

Aaaaagh!

ELIZABETH: Fearless Frobisher, we meet again.

FROBISHER falls to his knees, head bowed.

FROBISHER: Forgive me, Your Majesty. I was not informed of your presence in Friesland.

ELIZABETH: Naturally you were not informed. You are supposed to notice!

Stay!

Your pistol if you please Master Crowe.

CROWE is alarmed, but hands it over.

If one wishes to fell a beast, one must employ the laws of governance taught to me by my father. A firm arm, and a tender finger. Then squeeze. So.

She takes aim, fires the pistol offstage, in the direction of the 'beast'.

You see, a hit.

Offstage, a cry, prolongued and dying, becoming clearly human at the end. A pause, as all look in that direction.

How strange. That is a voice sounds familiar.

Enter WALSINGHAM, in his long fur coat; blood on his hand – and the tone of his voice – shows he is very hurt.

WALSINGHAM: Your Majesty….!? Your loyal servant! Shot!

He swoons. Lights down.

9

THE COURT OF BEASTS

A series of small, ringing 'pings'.

Lights up on the same place, or a similar place, some minutes later. WALSINGHAM is bent over ELIZABETH's knee, his head upstage, hidden from sight. ELIZABETH has a pair of large tweezers, borrowed from CROWE, with which she is yanking out gunshot from WALLY's backside. She flings each in turn into a bucket, held by FROBISHER – making the pinging noise which led into the scene. WALSINGHAM flinches and yelps with each piece removed. CROWE stands behind, keeping score.

ELIZABETH: Hold still Sir Francis, it will go…much better for you.

How many is that Master Crowe?

CROWE: Twenty-three Your Majesty.

ELIZABETH: Twenty-three?!

FROBISHER: I loaded birdshot, Your Majesty.

WALSINGHAM: Aaagh.

ELIZABETH: Hardly the stuff to stop a beast of Wally's proportions.

WALSINGHAM: Ow ow, Your Majesty.

ELIZABETH: It will take your mind off your toothache. Be grateful.

She tosses the next one high in the air. FROBISHER is equal to it, and the ping brings chuckles and smiles all the way round – except of course for WALLY – this is turning into a game…

Bravo, Master Frobisher!

FROBISHER: I am curious Your Majesty to know the reason for your arrival in Friesland – not that you are not most welcome.

He catches another high one – even trickier this time. Polite claps and congratulations all round – ELIZABETH is back in her court, and revelling in it, with a childish glee we've seen before.

ELIZABETH: What can I tell you, Captain…

Another ping. FROBISHER has to dive for this one. Cheers again, and he ends standing, wanting an answer.

FROBISHER: (*Prompting.*) Your Majesty?

ELIZABETH: Wally and I simply wish to check on the progress of our venture. Is that surprising?

FROBISHER: Not at all. I can inform you, Majesty, things are progressing very well.

ELIZABETH: Yes. I heard that from Master Crowe.

She tosses up another – and we hear the ping. This time, though, FROBISHER has not moved, so focussed is he on this new conversation, he has stopped playing the game.

Is there a problem, Captain?

FROBISHER: None Majesty. We have mined over a hundred tons of black earth – that will be almost fifty tons of gold for the royal coffers.

ELIZABETH: Really? And how many tons for you, in your extra ships?

FROBISHER looks sharply at CROWE.

In any case I am not concerned with racketeering. For one I expect no less from a pirate, for the other, I am informed there is no gold to be had from the rock. It is all quite useless.

If looks could kill, CROWE would certainly be dead. ELIZABETH applies some cream to WALLY's furry backside.

Ointment now Wally. Brace yourself.

FROBISHER: Your Majesty, Master Crowe is trained in the art of medicine. Barely that. He knows nothing of the science of metals. The rock must reach a great heat before it will part with its treasure. Then we can pour it into pots, make coins, jewellery and so forth…

ELIZABETH: And if you cannot get it hot enough? What then?

FROBISHER: We shall build bigger furnaces. In England.

ELIZABETH: At more expense to the crown, no doubt.

FROBISHER: There may be some…additional expenditure. But for a very great prize, Majesty, you'll agree.

The SHIP'S BOY gives a hacking cough.

SHIP'S BOY: Begging your pardon Ma'am. Captain.

He takes the rag to CROWE.

'Nother one for you Master Crowe.

CROWE takes the rag, to his own embarrassment and ELIZABETH's distaste. The SHIP'S BOY sits down again.

ELIZABETH: You were saying?

FROBISHER: We also plan to capture Esquimauxs. With whom Your Majesty may converse. Quwaaaahl.

ELIZABETH gives him a withering look.

ELIZABETH: I do solemnly swear, the next man I hear utter that word I shall pack in ice myself.

We invested a great deal in Friesland and so far all we have for our pains, are chilblains, frostbite, and sundry discomforts.

Poor Wally here has suffered a fate most violent. Is that not so Sir Francis?

WALSINGHAM: Indeed Majesty.

ELIZABETH: Up now Wally.

WALSINGHAM: Thank you my Lady.

ELIZABETH: You'll be sore for a while, I apologise for that.

WALSINGHAM: No no Your Majesty…

As he turns, we see the fur coat has in fact become a skin, and his mouth has sprouted tusks; WALLY has become a walrus.

...the pain will pass, as I am delighted to say, has my toothache.

What?

ELIZABETH: Captain, I wonder if you could arrange to break every looking-glass in Friesland?

WALSINGHAM: 'Break', the looking-glass Ma'am? Why 'break', the glass?

Why does everyone stare?

Everyone looks away, busying themselves.

Or look away?

Your Majesty, is something caught in my moustaches?

ELIZABETH: No Wally. I think I can say your whiskers have never looked finer.

WALSINGHAM: There is something concerning my appearance, I believe...

ELIZABETH: Master Crowe, you wish to be a physician. You will explain to Sir Francis the nature of his condition.

CROWE comes to the rescue – improvising as he goes...

CROWE: Sir Francis...has adapted to this place, very well, it seems.

WALSINGHAM: Adapted? How 'adapted'?

CROWE: He has begun to grow more...robust, stronger – you have become a more handsome creature altogether, one more suited to the conditions...as it were.

ELIZABETH: Oh very good.

Pause.

WALSINGHAM: More handsome? Well. Now my toothache's gone, I must say I'm feeling rather hungry. Shall I set about finding us all some quwaaahl majesty? There's a rather good ice hole I was making back there; on reflection, the water here is remarkably bright and clear, I'll go straight away…

ALL: NO!!!

ELIZABETH: There won't be time, Wally. It's my opinion, we should abandon this unnatural place as soon as we can. We shall journey homeward and hope all our…ill-effects wear off, before we land.

CROWE: I agree, Majesty. All those in favour?

There is a general 'aye'.

ELIZABETH: Master Crowe, when I wish to unleash the beast of democracy on Friesland, I will let you know. Till then, I remain your sovereign.

We'll leave.

FROBISHER: Your Majesty. Since you are so keen to abandon our enterprise before we finish, and since I am by your decree the named commander of this expedition – you will permit me to show you a wonder of the island.

A sight I have not allowed anyone here to see. Something that will teach Your Majesty the great value of what England has here.

ELIZABETH: Are we talking more rocks, Captain.

FROBISHER: No Majesty. This…this is a treasure far greater than any gold.

A pregnant pause.

SHIP'S BOY: Nah, let's go home.

General approval, all turn to leave – except ELIZABETH.

ELIZABETH: Hold. I shall go with the Captain.

WALSINGHAM: But Your Maj…

ELIZABETH: Your butt has recently escaped torment. Do not tempt me further. There is something in what the Captain says appeals to me. Lead on, Captain Frobisher.

FROBISHER: This way, Your Majesty.

ELIZABETH exits. FROBISHER waves his pistol at the rest in warning.

No one follows. You heard Her Majesty.

Firm arm, tender finger.

Exit FROBISHER. WALLY the walrus picks a piece of shot from the bucket, and examines it.

WALSINGHAM: Strange, unnatural land. I swear I've smelled this smell before.

Seal blubber.

He pops it in his mouth. Blackout.

10

THE BAY OF SOULS

Wind. The creaking ice.

Lights up on another place on the island. A flat sheet of ice, with a light covering of snow.

ELIZABETH and FROBISHER walk about it, their attention fixed on the surface of the ice, their feet occasionally scraping aside the snow.

ELIZABETH: This one?

FROBISHER: Robert Smedley. From Lancashire.

Pause.

ELIZABETH: This?

FROBISHER: Griffiths, Your Majesty. First Mate. His father John Griffiths, taught me everything I know. How to read the sea. How you should never try teaching the sea how to behave. How to swim.

ELIZABETH: You didn't swim before you went to sea?

FROBISHER: I was sent to sea by my guardian. Before that I was a landlubber, like the rest.

ELIZABETH: And this man?

FROBISHER: Harston. Charlie. My first Ship's Boy.

ELIZABETH: A pretty face. Hardly more than a child, with his golden locks.

Quite a collection. And a ghoulish one.

FROBISHER: A crew, Yer Majesty. All but entire. The ship disappeared. Lost her in the sea smoke, when we arrived in Friesland. Must have hit ice, or a whale. Now the crew are captured here, immortal. 'They saw the depths of the sea. Now they keep the watch.'

ELIZABETH: Extraordinary.

Though how you imagine this hall of mirrors, this graveyard, will convince me your project succeeds is beyond me, Captain. Quite the opposite.

FROBISHER: Not 'graveyard' Ma'am. I called this place the Bay of Souls. The Soul of England lies here. Spirits bent on England's glory. Elizabeth's Spain.

ELIZABETH: You flatter us both Frobisher. These men sought glory for themselves, not me.

FROBISHER: No empire was built without such men. You're right, the first men on these shores were plain men, men with hunger, with fire in their bellies. No one even knew the place existed till we came. They knew the risks, but sailed anyway, to where no Englishman had sailed before.

Some people like armchairs, to see the world in books. Master Crowe is one of them. You've seen the way he is, the real world terrifies him. Others find the shape of how things are, they go and look and chart and pace it out, and measure. If we turn back, we betray my lads. There'll be no empire for them, or us – Spain will rule the waves a thousand years.

When time froze for these boys, they were proud to be your subjects. They watch for shooting stars.

Offstage, noise of a struggle.

WALSINGHAM: (*Off.*) Get your hands off me Sir!! I warn you, I have a firm arm, and a tender…flipper! (*Realising the change.*) Aagh!

BO'SUN: (*Off.*) Stop him lads!

Enter WALLY the Walrus, carrying the musket in one flipper, a looking-glass in the other, pursued by the crew.

FROBISHER: Stop there fiend, or I fire!

ELIZABETH: Lower your gun Captain, that fiend is my Minister of State.

What is it Wally?

WALSINGHAM: Majesty!! I have become…a walrus!!!!

ELIZABETH: Indeed, Wally. You have. We all have our burdens to bear, but we must carry them bravely.

WALSINGHAM: But Your Majesty…

FROBISHER: He approaches Majesty…

FROBISHER's gun is levelled again.

ELIZABETH: Hold fire Captain… Wally, I am sorry for your trouble, indeed I am…

WALSINGHAM: But think, Majesty – when Your Majesty shot me, and injured me so horribly before…

ELIZABETH: An accident Wally, we thought you were the Beast…

WALSINGHAM: But Majesty – I was then a man. I distinctly recall, I had hands, teeth, a human's skin… I did not smell, hardly at all.

ELIZABETH: That's true.

BO'SUN: He stinks enough now.

ELIZABETH: That – is also true.

WALSINGHAM: But what can it mean, Majesty…?

ELIZABETH: It means you want a bath, Wally.

WALSINGHAM: No, think Your Majesty. You wounded not a walrus, I was then your Walsingham, your loyal servant! The voice of truth in the Royal Ear. What can this mean?

Beat.

ELIZABETH: I don't know what it means, Wally. Something to do with shooting the messenger, perhaps…

Anyway you are hardly the only one transformed. Captain Frobisher here has become a wolf – very appropriate.

It's true – FROBISHER finds he has sprouted the silvery tail of a timber wolf. The BO'SUN has orange stockings…

And you, Master Bo'sun, look most like a goose!

BO'SUN: Yer Majesty!

ELIZABETH: Though I don't recognise the boy, I must say.

MR WALKER: A squirrel!

ELIZABETH: And you, Mr Walker, a bear.

Pause as all inspect their plumage.

More exotic creatures than in my court.

All we need now is Master Crowe. Has anyone seen Master Crowe?

All look round to see CROWE enter, as a penguin. He stops still. He makes the only noise he can make.

CROWE: Quwaaahl.

ELIZABETH: Strange. I understood there are no penguins in the arctic.

SHIP'S BOY: Her Majesty's face!

ELIZABETH: My face…?

SHIP'S BOY: All white! You…yer a snowy owl, Yer Majesty…

BO'SUN: No, no – the arctic lemming…

MR WALKER: No not a lemming – the arctic fox.

A long low creak begins that will build through the next few lines. FROBISHER is the first to hear it, and looks at his feet…

FROBISHER: Majesty…

ELIZABETH: Not now Captain… A fox? Aren't they quite vicious? Wally, what do you say?

FROBISHER: (*Referring to the noise.*) Yer Majesty, the ice…

WALSINGHAM: Not fox – Her Majesty is not so small…though she is very clever…

MR WALKER: …and sly, Your Majesty.

BO'SUN: Clever as a lemming?

MR WALKER: Much cleverer than a goose.

WALSINGHAM: Or a squirrel, then…

SHIP'S BOY: No, *I'm* a squirrel…

BO'SUN: Well she must be something.

WALSINGHAM: Some kind of small gazelle, perhaps?

MR WALKER: In the arctic?

CROWE: Quwaaahl.

BO'SUN: You can talk…

ELIZABETH: Quiet!

What is quite clear, is, your queen asked you for gold, and instead you've all become…become…

SHIP'S BOY: Sick, Your Majesty.

ELIZABETH: Uh, you little beast, now I've lost my thread completely!

SHIP'S BOY: (*Coughing.*) I'm sick, I'm very sick…I'm dying, aren't I Master Crowe? I hear angels…

BO'SUN: Angels?!

ELIZABETH: Shhhhh! I hear it too. Not angels. Why Master Crowe, I do believe… I did not think to hear it…I did not think to ever hear the Esquimaux sing…

The ethereal sound of Esquimaux singing. Snow begins to fall. All stand, wonderstruck. Lights shrink the ice to an island. A distant bell begins to toll, and the ice groans again…snow falls as the scene begins to transform…

11

JUDGEMENT

A bell tolls. Cheers.

Lights up on the Queen's chamber in the palace at Windsor, one week after Scene 1.

Centre-stage, a low couch, covered with a scarlet blanket.

ELIZABETH in full rig stands upstage, at the open window, her back to the audience, waving her handkerchief to the crowds below.

DEVEREUX offstage, calls to her.

DEVEREUX: (*Off.*) Your Majesty! Your Majesty!

Enter DEVEREUX, running. He is dressed identically, ie as ELIZABETH, though dishevelled.

Your Majesty!

ELIZABETH turns around, and we see it is WALSINGHAM, also dressed as ELIZABETH. He/she jumps at the sight of DEVEREUX/ ELIZABETH.

WALSINGHAM: My Lord Devereux! What is the meaning of this?

DEVEREUX: I mean to ask the same of you, Sir.

WALSINGHAM: Close the window, quickly!

DEVEREUX snaps the window closed, and comes downstage.

I ask again, what is the meaning of this?

DEVEREUX: Again, Sir, I ask the same.

A moment. They simultaneously reach for pieces of paper in their pocket/sleeve – like gunfighters at the OK Corral. DEVEREUX is fastest on the draw.

DEVEREUX: Friday! Friday, I am Elizabeth!

WALSINGHAM: Fri…can it really be Friday already? Oh dear…

DEVEREUX doesn't try too hard to hide his exasperation.

Perhaps…perhaps not many people saw you, my Lord.

DEVEREUX: Perhaps not. Leaving out the hundreds assembled on the dockside to wave, the four dozen merchants to whom I gave my hand at the celebration breakfast, and the four hundred thousand gathered below your window here…hardly any saw their monarch at all today.

WALSINGHAM: Well then, perhaps not many people saw us *both.* There's hope there, I'm certain.

DEVEREUX: Yes, and then the multitude will argue over which did see us: Thomas will say, I saw Her Majesty at the dockside, and John will say, Liar! Scoundrel! It was me who saw the Queen waving at Windsor. And then the fighting starts.

WALSINGHAM: It was ever the case my Lord, one kingdom, two queens, all ends most bloody and foul – why did I not check my diary?

They sit down side by side, defeated.

Oh my Lord Devereux. This has been quite the worst week of my life.

DEVEREUX: Aye, Sir Francis. And mine. Which is sad, as it is to be my last.

ELIZABETH: I can honestly say, it has not been too hot for me.

ELIZABETH has appeared in the doorway to her bedchamber. She is dressed in her bedclothes, and a dressing gown, and does not look amused. The 'ELIZABETHS' drop to their knees.

WALSINGHAM / DEVEREUX: Your Majesty!!

Enter DR BURCOT – an ancient, wearing a skullcap, and carrying a tray. He also wears orange stockings. He rattles his way oblivious to all, toward the couch, centre-stage.

DR BURCOT: How is our sickly monarch this morning, mmmm?

He lifts the corner of the scarlet blanket. Nothing.

Most strange. I certainly left her here…

He looks up, and sees the two ELIZABETHS. He jumps slightly.

Your Maj…. Oh my wondrous tonic…! *Two* sickly monarchs…! Good morning Your Majesties…

ELIZABETH clears her throats, he turns.

Ah…Your Majesty – again! *Three* sickly monarchs…!

ELIZABETH: Walsingham. I demand explanation!

DR BURCOT: Allow me, Your Majesty. It appears, I have invented a tonic of multiplication….!!!

WALSINGHAM: Your Majesty, this is Dr Burcot. He has been attending Your Majesty during a terrible illness…

ELIZABETH: So I gather. Was the illness his or mine?

WALSINGHAM: I assure you, he is a very distinguished physician my Lady, the best in the land…

ELIZABETH: Nonsense. He's the Bo'sun, I'd know him anywhere. He's certainly no physician. Though he is certainly a quack.

DR BURCOT: A quack!?

ELIZABETH: To be particular, a goose. A barnacle goose. Very common in the arctic. Look at his legs, if you will not believe it. (*Responding to their bemusement.*) What?

Beat.

DR BURCOT: (*To WALSINGHAM.*) Perhaps if I were to reverse the cordial, Your Majesty…

WALSINGHAM: It is so wonderful to see you awake Your Majesty. Every morning for a week we brought the looking-glass near. Hoping for a mist, a fog to show you lived…

DR BURCOT: And now this! Life abundant! How long has England prayed for Her Majesty to multiply! No wonder the bells are ringing!

ELIZABETH: Sir Francis, have this man removed from our presence, before I divide him myself.

WALSINGHAM: At once Your Majesty. This way good Doctor…

DR BURCOT: Now now Your Majesty, I must tell you sternly – all three of Your Majesties – you must prepare yourself for a shock. You have suffered a nasty dose of the pox, recovery cannot be hurried.

ELIZABETH: The what?!

WALSINGHAM: The smallpox my Lady, a dreadful and deadly disease…

DR BURCOT: I was forced to fall back on a remedy most ancient…

WALSINGHAM: …which involved a most interesting dressing, my Lady.

ELIZABETH: So I see.

DR BURCOT: 'Wrap the patient in a robe of scarlet…place the patient by a hot fire…treat the patient with sundry powerful tonics…then wait. In the passage of time, the patient will revive magnificent. Or die. Most painful.'

Certainly not the work of a quack, young Lady.

ELIZABETH: I knew it, I was poisoned, that damnable seal blubb… Did he say smallpox?

WALSINGHAM: No my Lady. That was me.

ELIZABETH: Mirror. Looking-glass, quickly.

A mirror is passed to the panicking queen. WALSINGHAM is in oily mode.

WALSINGHAM: There, Your Majesty. Your skin has remained remarkably unblemished, as you plainly see…

ELIZABETH: Yes. I do think you're right. I see no blemish at all.

DR BURCOT: Is Her Majesty short-sighted…?

WALSINGHAM: Not at all Dr Burcot.

DR BURCOT: I do have a preparation for weak-sightedness…

WALSINGHAM: My Lady's eyes remain as pure of defect, as does the alabaster surface of her skin Dr Burcot, will you not say it.

DR BURCOT: What? Oh – yes, yes, indeed. Like the driven snow, Majesty. At least, nothing a little more white lead cannot hide…

ELIZABETH: Then I am unharmed. We thank you kindly Dr Burcot for your service to us. You must let us give you a house, a county, or something.

DR BURCOT: No no. It is reward enough for your servant, to know unimaginable wealth will flow from the sale of patents.

Now, if Your Majesties will permit me to leave your presence, I will continue my work right away.

DR BURCOT: Your Majesty…

Your Majesty…

Majesty…

Having bowed to each in turn, he turns at the door for one last thought.

You should not thank me entirely for your recovery, Your Majesties. Thank the owner of the scarlet robe…a young man who was here many times, and did mop your brow most attentive. That was before you were a tri-une queen, when you were still a mono-arch, in fact…

Quite marvellous.

Having surveyed his handiwork, he exits. DEVEREUX throws himself at ELIZABETH's feet.

DEVEREUX: Your Majesty – I am your most humble servant. I do most humbly beg for your mercy…

ELIZABETH: Quiet. Pass the robe to me.

The scarlet blanket is passed to ELIZABETH. She holds it tenderly for a moment, before demanding an explanation from WALSINGHAM.

Well?

WALSINGHAM: (*Swallowing hard.*) Your Majesty, when your malady was discovered I thought it vital to prevent a general panic – the people feel Your Majesty's absence so

cruelly. There were acts of state to attend, engagements to
fulfil. I resolved to appear *for* Her Majesty.

And at the same time, there being occasions where *I* must
be seen not simply *as* Her Majesty, but be seen *with* Her
Majesty, someone intimate with my Lady's manner was
required – a fellow who knew as well as I the sweet smile,
sharp wit, the keen intelligence, your most legendary
generosity – and someone dropped the name of Lord
Devereux in my ear, and I released him. Then, when…(Dr
Burcot…)

ELIZABETH: Enough.

That creature there. Are you saying that is Lord Devereux?

DEVEREUX: Indeed, Majesty, and my tongue pants now in
earnest for your mercy.

ELIZABETH: Then the mad Doctor is right, my sight is flawed.
I know I sent that traitor to the Tower. That he might forfeit
his head.

WALSINGHAM: You did, Majesty, but, as I said, in the
circum…

ELIZABETH: There is skating on the inside of my skull!

WALSINGHAM: I'm sorry…?

ELIZABETH: Hold your tongue Sir, or become a walrus!

DEVEREUX: Your Majesty, I beg you now, if you did ever
love your Devereux, do not send him back to the Tower. If
there is anything in heaven or on earth your servant might
do…

ELIZABETH: (*Fierce and forbidding.*) My Lord of Essex. I'll not
shrink from kingly duty, however much you plead. I know
I have the body of a weak and feeble woman, but I assure
you, I have the heart and stomach of a king.

WALSINGHAM: That is very good…has Your Majesty worked this speech…(before?)

ELIZABETH: My words come direct from God.

It seems I have had a dream. A most rare vision. And in that dream I have mused upon many things. I have concluded that to execute a traitor – while just and right by the law of this land and though approved by ancient practice of kings – may be a price I should not exact upon myself. Having consulted a Crowe, who became a penguin, I have determined I shall be human, with a heart that beats. And can be gentle. You may keep your head my Lord…

DEVEREUX: Your Majesty…(I know you will not regret it.)

ELIZABETH: …but not on my pillow. That would cost more than any queen should pay. And certainly any woman. Go to your wife, your rich widow, and never come near us. Never.

DEVEREUX: Your Majesty…

ELIZABETH: Go. Let our love be struck from the record. We will say that I remained a virgin. Or something.

DEVEREUX approaches to kiss the royal hand, but ELIZABETH turns her back. He leaves. A long pause. ELIZABETH speaks quietly…

Since I am raised from my sickbed, I shall be Queen.

WALSINGHAM: Yes, Your Majesty.

ELIZABETH: Those bells that rang. What do they announce?

WALSINGHAM: They rang for Captain Frobisher, my Lady. A celebration of his launch for the Arctic.

ELIZABETH: You mean his return, surely.

WALSINGHAM: No Majesty. Captain Frobisher and his fleet sailed from Dartford only this morning. We – I – you, have great hopes for Frobisher; he will bring us back much gold. In fact, I took the liberty while you slept – that is, you took the liberty – of doubling Her Majesty's personal investment in the light of Frobisher's latest forecast. I myself have sold several properties, throwing the proceeds entirely into the venture. Let the Spanish have their Americas. England will be the greatest power in Europe by the Spring. Would you not say so Your Majesty?

Do you not as I do, pant for their return? Do you not, as I, ache to behold those heaps of black, Black Earth, piled high on Tilbury's docks?

Do you not?

Majesty?

Ma'am?

What.

ELIZABETH: HA!!!

WALSINGHAM: Is Your Majesty quite well?

ELIZABETH laughs uncontrollably…while WALSINGHAM dithers…

Majesty…? Shall I call Dr Burcot…?

She is beginning to sober…

ELIZABETH: Oh Wally. How apt a name that is.

WALSINGHAM: You mean, 'Burcot', my Lady?

She sobers.

ELIZABETH: I mean Wally. There is no gold to be found in the Black Earth, not a drop.

(*A list.*) I now know beyond doubt that Captain Frobisher, is a mugger with a ship. *My* ship. His Black Earth is about as full of gold, as my aching teeth. Master Crowe's Esquimaux will stay alive only as long as we stay at home. And you Walsingham, have just waved farewell to a great deal of money. *My* money.

WALSINGHAM: You know this, my Lady…?

ELIZABETH: Yes Wally, I believe I do.

WALSINGHAM: Of a certainty, Majesty?

ELIZABETH: Beyond doubting.

> *WALSINGHAM picks up his ginger wig and makes for the window.*

WALSINGHAM: Then, if Her Majesty will permit me to impersonate her one final time…I shall call back the fleet immediately…

ELIZABETH: No Sir, you will not! Come away from the window, Wally. Else I will shoot.

WALSINGHAM: You have no musket, Your Majesty.

ELIZABETH: Very well I shall have you hanged, I'm not greatly concerned with the manner of your dispatch.

WALSINGHAM: But but Your Majesty…

ELIZABETH: Skating, Sir Francis!

WALSINGHAM: Skates be damned my Lady! If there is no gold in Black Earth, England will be the laughing stock of Europe! The City of London invested thousands of pounds! Your own fortune, your prestige will be horribly damaged! The torment of your servants will be for nothing!

ELIZABETH: My decision will not be changed. My word is law.

WALSINGHAM: But…I do not understand, Ma'am. Why?

ELIZABETH: Because Francis, I have discovered there is Frobisher's Gold in us all. Rather a lot of it. We hope to find some treasure there. Just as we hope and go on hoping that somewhere, out there, there is a new land filled with gold. A land of exotic creatures and new words and effortless profit. Where young men discover the true meaning of courage, and the natives they mug are enriched by the experience. Where Englishmen do not always become beasts. It is possible there may not be such a land. But where does that leave us? Here. On this dank little island, with only ourselves to ruin. And so we must set sail, again and again. As long as we are England. As long as there is a world to win, and someone to come second.

You did well to wave Frobisher off. I would have done the same. History will no doubt say I did. Elizabeth took her 'kerchief and waved goodbye to her explorers and wished them the very best of grace. Godspeed! For England! And they were gone. A square of sail, the dying cheers, across, over, beyond the edge of the known, to the unknown, those brave few, and on.

We will not dwell upon the torment of our heroes, no more than on the suffering of the peoples they conquer. England will have her place in the world. And I will brook no quibbling at the cost.

Now, Sir Francis, the future can come to us.

Pause. WALSINGHAM is inwardly shaken, seeing for the first time the creature he has created. ELIZABETH inspects her teeth in the looking-glass.

Do we have any sweets Wally?

WALSINGHAM: We do my Lady.

A very long slow fade of the light begins as WALLY finds a huge box of sweets…

These were sent by the Duke of Anjou, who I think, my Lady, now firmly considers himself your suitor.

ELIZABETH: (*Smiling.*) Does he indeed. Does he have a good leg?

WALSINGHAM: He has an excellent leg, my Lady. The Duke is, in every way, an excellent prospect.

ELIZABETH: I have proved an excellent student to you, have I not, Wally. The beauty, and the beast.

WALSINGHAM: Indeed you have, Majesty.

ELIZABETH: In days to come, I fancy we will achieve great things together.

ELIZABETH pops a sweet into her mouth, and chews for a moment. A sharp intake of breath from ELIZABETH; she holds her jaw, then smiles.

Don't be alarmed, Wally. Only a twinge.

Blackout.

The End.